Supergrowth Companies

Supergrowth Companies
Entrepreneurs in
Action

John Harrison and Bernard Taylor

WITH

Ann Todd and Mahen Tampoe

Butterworth-Heinemann
Linacre House, Jordan Hill, Oxford OX2 8DP
A division of Reed Educational and Professional Publishing Ltd

 A member of the Reed Elsevier plc group

OXFORD   BOSTON   JOHANNESBURG
MELBOURNE   NEW DELHI   SINGAPORE

First published 1996
Reprinted 1997

British Library Cataloguing in Publication Data
A catalogue record for this book is available from the British Library.

ISBN 0 7506 2750 6

Typeset by David Gregson Associates, Beccles, Suffolk
Printed and bound in Great Britain by Clays Ltd, St Ives plc

Contents

Acknowledgements

We would like to acknowledge the many individuals and organizations who have helped to develop the research upon which this book is based. The main contributors are listed below.

Professor Dietger Hahn, Doctor Ulrich Gräb and their colleagues at the Justus Liebig University carried out the research in Germany. This study, together with the original UK research was sponsored by the Anglo-German Foundation.

The basic research for the study of high growth mid-size companies in Britain was conducted by a number of mature students and researchers on the MBA and doctoral programmes at the Henley Management College. The work was started in 1985 by Stephen E. Palmer who produced and analysed the first database. The work was continued by Armand Gilinsky who wrote the report on the UK research for the Anglo-German Foundation and made comparisons with corresponding medium size companies in the USA. Adrian Hilmi produced the comparison between the results for British companies and those for their German counterparts.

Christopher D. Emin, Lesley Hughes, George Laverty and Edward Mackenzie performed the database analyses and conducted the field interviews with chief executives which examined the international strategies of growth companies, an enquiry that was sponsored by Price Waterhouse. Martin Wyn Griffith and Martin Laycock conducted recent studies of specific industries.

We would like to pay a special tribute to Professor Peter Herbert of Henley Management College for the original inspiration for the work. It was he who first identified the special interest of mid-size high growth companies and recognized the extraordinary contribution that they make to the creation of wealth, employment and innovation in the UK and other economies. Peter has been a continuing inspiration, particularly in his role in preparing the shortlist for the Business Enterprise Award.

We would like to thank our two sponsors, the Anglo-German Foundation, who sponsored the initial work, and Price Waterhouse, who sponsored the work on the international strategies of growing British companies.

Finally, we would like to say how much we have appreciated the continued interest and cooperation of more than one hundred chief executives who have given their time and talked very candidly about their strategies and leadership styles. We would like to dedicate this book to them.

John Harrison, Bernard Taylor,
Ann Todd and Mahen Tampoe
Henley, September 1995

Foreword

This book is about success – about a group of entrepreneurs who have created companies which have grown to dominate their markets in a relatively short period of time and about the strategies they have adopted. Based upon fifteen years of research, it is heartening to see that enterprise has been alive and well, even during periods of recession. Indeed, this alone should make the book required reading for those policy-makers who constantly bemoan our lack of capability in this arena. In particular, it dispels the popular British myth of the enthusiastic, uneducated amateur starting a business which they are then unable to manage. These 'new leaders' are professionally trained with a 'theory of the business' and a 'clear vision of the future' – but this has not constrained them! Like many of us, they have spotted a window of opportunity, usually in a niche market, but unlike most of us they have acted on it.

Throughout the case studies which are presented we begin to see themes emerging. These entrepreneurs are not media stars – it is not a necessary condition for success. They have simply got on with the job. They understand their market and its customers, the fragility of new ventures, the need for constant monitoring of the health of the business through 'bus ticket' controls, and they are able to assemble a talented and highly motivated team. Above all, the key word which runs throughout the book is 'flexibility' – the ability to adapt to changing market conditions almost at the drop of a hat. In short, they know their business.

This is not to suggest that it has been easy. Managing super-growth requires courage and a firm hand, and not all are successful. Moreover, whilst the generic strategies identified are intuitively appealing – diversification and international expansion, innovation, the search for excellence – they require a team which can translate these grand and overworked words into action. It also requires some element of luck.

I like this study. Based upon strong empirical evidence, it contains important insights for all those interested and involved in the world of enterprise. Certainly, it enhances our understanding of a sector critical to the health of the economy. However, for me, the most encouraging part of all is its optimism. It is saying to executives in large organizations, and to students from all disciplines – you CAN do it. Education is not a fatal wound but an advantage. You should be careful, but it is not too late. Hurray!

Sue Birley, July 1996

Introduction

Henley, September 1995

This book is about what we have termed *supergrowth businesses* – the medium-sized high-growth businesses that provide much of the momentum for real national economic growth. In particular they span the gap between the seed-corn new business start-ups and the large corporations that have the size and power to compete globally, but which frequently find innovation difficult. These vital supergrowth companies therefore both create new corporations in their own right and provide the acquisition targets that large corporations use to refresh their business ideas, management teams and competitive edge.

Who is this book for?

The book has been aimed at three different audiences. The first group comprises any business managers seeking to create growth and promote corporate development. Within this group are entrepreneurs and owners of business wishing both to emulate the success of the business leaders featured in our sample of high-growth companies and to avoid their mistakes. This group also includes managers of small or medium-sized businesses or those in influential positions within divisions of large companies who are interested in business growth and corporate development. A significant section of the book is also specifically directed at those managers wishing to grow their business internationally.

The next group consists of students of business growth such as those undertaking MBAs or managers undertaking executive programmes on corporate development.

The third group are researchers investigating growth businesses who are concerned with the contribution that these businesses can make to wealth creation, employment and innovation.

What is a supergrowth company?

The most visible examples of such companies in Britain have been those run by well-known entrepreneurs such as Richard Branson of Virgin, Andrew Lloyd Webber of the Really Useful Group, Anita Roddick of the Body Shop and Alan Sugar of Amstrad. But these companies represent only the tip of the iceberg – there are many more equally successful supergrowth businesses whose leaders have adopted a lower profile. In order to identify supergrowth businesses it was necessary for us to set ourselves some base qualifying criteria; these are listed in

---

The criteria for 'supergrowth'

1. Turnover between £10 million and £100 million in the core study period.

2. Growth in both sales and profits of at least 20 per cent per annum in the core period.

3. Sectors where profits come largely from 'deals' rather than from regular trading were excluded (e.g. property dealing, banking and financial services).

4. No companies were included that had recently suffered losses in two consecutive years (in order to eliminate turn-around businesses). Nevertheless companies were included that were undergoing 'rejuvenation' and a number of well-known family businesses fell into this category.

5. The growth generated had to arise mainly from organic growth rather than by acquisition.

6. The sample was restricted to entire businesses (i.e. sub-sidiaries were excluded).

---

the box.

From time to time companies have been included in the super-growth study sample which have not fully complied with the criteria, but which have demonstrated characteristics of typical supergrowth companies.

The challenge

As Britain's economy has gone through successive 'boom and bust' the supergrowth companies have been walking a difficult tightrope. High growth brings financial vulnerability and stretches management resources – it can be like holding a tiger by the tail. But the lessons offered by the winning teams provide an important information source for any manager wishing to create or contribute to a successful growth business whether it be large, medium or small in size, an independent company or a subsidiary or division of a larger corporation.

In several cases the supergrowth businesses studied have

become world class competitors. Using their experiences we studied the strategic actions leading to superior competitive performance such as:

- benchmarking world class standards,
- focusing on areas where you have an 'unfair advantage',
- creating 'federations' of little companies to create larger scale,
- coping with global competition,
- dealing with new technologies and new market opportunities, and
- expanding into international markets.

We were interested in what successful growth businesses do, and where some fail.

The research base which underpins this book has been assembled by successive teams at Henley Management College. The first study period began in 1979/80 and since then a substantial long-term database of these businesses has been created which is still being added to. In that time over 200 companies have been studied and a large number of company executives interviewed. Many detailed case studies have been prepared – more than 50 in the UK and over 20 in Germany – reflecting specific experiences. The basic question being asked throughout has been 'How do these companies survive and grow in a rapidly changing market place?'

The content of the book

Part 1 of the book starts with the results of the most recent studies of leading supergrowth companies. The first chapter shows how a struggling engineering company has been transformed into a successful world class competitor. The second profiles a number of successful supergrowth businesses in the entertainment industry – a sector where the UK has achieved considerable international success – and illustrates how successful businesses operate in the growing service sector. Then the third chapter deals with the ways in which supergrowth companies dealt with the onset of the recent recession. It focuses the strategies that have led to survival and growth in the cycle of boom and recession and provides a checklist for survival.

Part 2 deals with the detailed studies that have been carried out over the years into how the supergrowth companies succeed. Each chapter is based on a key part of the success story. The role of the entrepreneur and the leader was one obvious area that warranted close attention and is featured in one chapter. We were also keen to understand how management dealt with the following areas, each of which forms the subject of a chapter:

- How do you overcome the barriers to growth (and avoid the pitfalls)?
- What are the key success factors for a supergrowth business?
- How do you develop growth strategies which allow you to seize and exploit the available opportunities?

These chapters are then followed by the results of research studies that provide a different perspective. Chapter 9 pays specific attention to the problems of creating supergrowth companies in the the service sector. This is followed in Chapter 10 by analysis of how the equivalent German supergrowth businesses differ from their UK counterparts.

Part 3 deals with the specific issues concerned with growing international businesses. At some point most growing businesses are faced with the opportunity to expand overseas. For some this provides a huge additional opportunity, for others it has been a disaster. We have been able to identify those strategic approaches that have proven successful in developing an international company.

The final section contains appendices which outline the research approaches and contain details of the resulting databases.

Although the results reported in this book are based on some 15 years of academic research, the aim has always been to stay in the realms of the practical. The emphasis is always on what people have done – what actions worked, and what didn't. Despite the fact that the study has been complex with over 200 businesses in many different sectors, each with its own levels of technology and its different approaches to the various issues faced, we have attempted to demonstrate the common features and experiences. In this way we hope that our readers can learn directly from others' experience and not be faced with a plethora of academic theory.

Part 1
Survival and success in boom and recession

Part 1 contains our latest studies on supergrowth companies. It starts with a case study of a successful 'metal bashing' business – a story of how business success can be achieved against the odds and in an unfashionable sector if the leadership is right. This is followed in Chapter 2 by a profile of supergrowth company success in a sector where Britain has a number of world class businesses – the entertainment industry. Chapter 3 shows how many of the companies that we have been tracking for some time dealt with the recession of the the late 1980s and early 1990s. It provides some clear lessons for success in midsize high-growth companies when the going is tough.

The chapters in this part are:

Chapter 1
Tallent Engineering – world class 'metal bashing'
How a management team created a world class business against all the odds.

Chapter 2
Putting on the top hat – entrepreneurs in entertainment
A profile of growth businesses in one of Britain's top export industries.

Chapter 3
Surviving the recession
How the supergrowth companies of the 1980s have fared when faced with the recession.

Tallent Engineering– world class 'metal bashing' 1

In recent years City financiers have veered away from investments in engineering and metal fabrication. After the decline of whole sectors like the British motorcycle and shipbuilding industries and key engineering businesses like British Leyland, it was generally believed that the British could not compete with the Japanese, the Germans and then the Koreans in 'metal bashing'.

This chapter tells the remarkable story of Tallent Engineering, a company which grew from a standing start in 1981 to a turnover of £60 million in 1993/94 against all the odds. A 1992 IBM Consultants/London Business School survey judged Tallent to be one of only 2 per cent of British manufacturing companies currently achieving standards which are *world class*.

Background

In the 1970s Tallent Engineering was a small but well established engineering business with a special competence in heavy metal pressings. The firm's main customer was its parent company, the Colston Group – manufacturers of domestic appliances. In 1979 the parent group decided that, as Britain's smallest domestic appliance manufacturing business, they could neither command economies of scale nor offer sufficient product differentiation, to compete with firms like Hoover, Hotpoint and Zanussi. The parent company therefore sold the appliance business to the Italian manufacturer Ariston, under an agreement by which they would receive royalties for their patented designs.

Initially, Tallent was able to replace much of its lost Colston business with work for the Talbot motor assembly plant in Linwood, Scotland, but problems were pending as by 1981, over 50 per cent of the £2 million output was going to Linwood and there were rumours that this plant was about to close as part of a world-wide rationalization programme.

At the beginning of the 1980s the company was therefore facing a bleak future, with its existing work base under threat and few obvious opportunities for new work as the recession deepened. The company had a turnover of less than £1.5 million in 1981/82 and was loss making. But by 1993/94 Tallent Engineering was firmly established as a mid-size high-growth business with a turnover of £60 million and profits in excess of £5 million (see Figure 1.1). The question we were interested in was: 'How did the company achieve this result in a declining industry (metal bashing) and in a period of difficult trading conditions?'

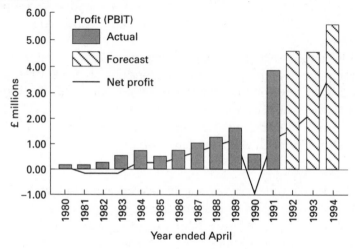

Figure 1.1 Tallent Holdings plc – trading performance.

Leadership, vision and focus

In 1980 Tallent appointed Bernard Robinson as the managing director of a new management team. Unlike many other businesses facing a similar situation, Tallent did not go outside for their new MD but instead chose someone who had joined the company as an apprentice tool-maker in 1956 and had worked his way up through the company. Bernard Robinson had become a production supervisor in 1965, works manager in 1972 and on his appointment as director in 1977 took night classes in order to obtain an accountancy qualification so that he could 'understand the numbers'.

It was clear to the new team that the firm had a one-off

chance to find a new long-term business opportunity before the Talbot business ceased. It was reckoned that a two-year 'window of opportunity' existed to make this happen. On examining the business Bernard Robinson found the status as follows:

We had a strong asset base, good freehold buildings, room to expand, some useful plant and machinery. Morale at the time was quite low but we had a loyal and committed workforce and some valuable core skills in areas such as pressing and basic engineering.

But they also had no real competitive edge; they were not low-cost producers, had no specific contracting edge, and no meaningful differentiation in product or process from their competitors. With the closure of their main past and present customers they also lacked any strategic direction or business focus.

Robinson was able to provide the business with a vision for the future. This was for a business based on superior quality and price over competition. He had visited Germany and Japan and seen better organized production linked with engineering skills in the former and robotics and new production process in the latter. Among the factors he observed were the close attention to quality, the close co-operation between design and engineering, and the close links between customers and suppliers. He also noted the increasing effects of globalization on industries such as the motor industry and the changing nature of the industry. He could see that despite the existing turmoil in the British car industry and the general over-capacity in Europe, fundamental changes were occurring which would provide opportunities for suppliers who could deliver low-cost and high-quality components.

Tallent's management team reviewed a broad range of industries such as consumer electronics, information technology and DIY, in order to seek manufacturing opportunities. The problem was that most potential markets required short-run efficiency to meet frequent model and specification changes, and it was felt that this was not the best route for Tallent. Eventually it appeared that the motor industry presented the best potential despite the turmoil that existed at the time. As Bernard Robinson stated:

We didn't just look at Britain. We looked at Europe and beyond. We looked at the world-wide direction of motor manufacturing and considered the possible future structure of the industry. We saw that the Japanese influence was making its presence felt almost everywhere. It was even then being rumoured that the Japanese might set up factories in Britain.

It was quite clear that Tallent could only play a part in the future motor manufacturing industry if it adopted radically different engineering and production methods.

We'd need to achieve consistently high quality if we were to succeed, we'd have to reorientate ourselves, get the workforce to accept new practices and adopt a policy of greater involvement in the business.

The company decided that they would seek high-volume work suited to their core pressing and engineering skills with long and uninterrupted production runs. This was then expressed as a statement of business focus:

We decided that chassis/structural components for mid-market, non-specialist cars were what we required. Such models tended to have 5-10 year lives, sell in volume and typically have chassis and sub-frames which remain unchanged although body and interior updating may occur.

Selling the vision to potential customers

It is one thing to create the vision, but quite another to sell it to potential customers. Tallent's management team knew that Rover (then part of British Leyland) were planning to launch new models and that Ford were at the design stage with the new Sierra. In the case of Rover, they presented their skills, their plans for the future, and by quoting competitive prices, persuaded them to give Tallent an initial order to make cross-members for the new SDI model. Through delivery performance the firm was able to increase its share of cross-member production from 30 per cent to 50 per cent and then to 100 per cent of Rover's requirements.

In order to obtain more of this type of business the company presented to Ford how they were adopting the latest manufacturing technologies, including robotics from Japan and software from Scandinavia, in order to deliver high volume, high quality and low cost.

At a visit to the Tallent's Aycliffe site in 1981, the team from

Ford were impressed with the management's commitment and the dedication of the workforce. They therefore awarded Tallent a contract to supply 800 000 pairs of rear suspension arms – a contract worth £20 million over four years. Soon afterwards they were able to negotiate additional work with the Rover group.

The board were keen to restrict their output for the motor manufacturing sector to not more than 50 per cent of annual sales in the early stages. They therefore also sought to develop orders from other locally based firms such as Thorn Lighting, Black & Decker and IBM in order to build some non-automotive businesses.

Developing the manufacturing capability

It was clear to the board that manufacturing quality would need to be a key contributor towards business success. Bernard Robinson had seen the way that quality permeates Japanese businesses and was determined to emulate their best practices. This started with operators being given the power to control the quality of their own output. It was also recognized that entire factory processes would need to be reviewed and changed. From his previous experience of shop floor practices Bernard Robinson knew that a series of organizational changes would need to be made and that this would be subject to resistance from employees.

Many of the processes used in Japan were quite alien to the traditional British engineering approach. Knowing the workforce well and acknowledging their low morale, I realized that the introduction of these new processes would take time. Much patience and training would be necessary. I and my board and production colleagues did a lot of 'management by walking about' in those days. We needed to think the entire production processes through and to decide what changes would be feasible, and how best they could be implemented.

This careful approach to the introduction of *Japanese production techniques* is in marked contrast to some other manufacturing businesses where the introduction of Japanese style working has been abandoned as not being suitable for Western businesses. It has become clear that just as the Japanese had to adapt the original US-based theories to suit their own culture,

7

firms wishing to adopt Japanese methods also have to adapt the methods to suit Western conditions.

A typical example of an area which can easily go wrong is in the introduction of *robotics*. The initial introduction of robots at Aycliffe was rightly and typically treated with a mixture of fear and scepticism. As Bernard Robinson confirms:

> They thought the machines were going to take their jobs. But we were able to disprove that theory quite quickly – there is actually plenty of room for both men and machines in modern manufacturing – so long as you get the blend right and use the machines for the right reasons. I had learned from my visits to Japan and elsewhere that human beings are best at tasks that call for variety and that modern computer-controlled machines are far better at repetitive tasks. The machines, once properly set up and maintained, produce what is wanted, when it is wanted with virtually no need for re-work.

Once the teething problems had been sorted out, the inspection process was built into the system. The workforce could then be directed to the critical areas between the machines and could concentrate on improving work flows and overall efficiencies. The concept of *continuing improvement* was also introduced – a concept that Bernard Robinson remains passionate about.

Strong positive leadership with clear direction and good communication has been a feature of the company's management style. Worker participation and employee involvement have also been encouraged. There are productivity and bonus schemes which have helped contribute to increasing productivity and the strike free record. The natural fear of the workforce's displacement by machines proved to be groundless as employee numbers grew from 150 in 1980 to over 700 in 1993. In fact the firm reckoned that during the 1980s every new robot installed created five new jobs. The workers are organized in customer-focused cells, and they are encouraged to suggest improvements at any time.

Financing the growth

The major difference between this type of business and the service businesses featured in many of our high-growth studies is the need for finance. Service businesses tend to be good cash generators and require relatively little capital investment or working capital. They can therefore keep borrowings and gearing low. Modern manufacturing businesses by contrast tend to be capital intensive with significant investments in high-technology plant and equipment and a large amount of working capital tied up in raw materials, parts, sub-assemblies and stocks of finished goods, as well as in debtors.

Tallent's expansion plans required a sizeable injection of *new capital* for modernization. Neither Tallent nor its parent company had the £3.5 million (one and a half times annual turnover) necessary to complete the first phase of modernization. The 1981–82 business plan document highlighted the need for additional capital and Alex Worrall the finance director was given the task of exploring the funding options.

It was recognized that a critical factor in the achievement of the funding would be the building up of credibility with banks, other potential investors and customers. Everyone had to be convinced of the firm's commitment to the business plan and their ability to deliver it. Part of the financial strategy was to get agencies like the Department of Trade and Industry actively involved by explaining the plans to them and seeking their active advice.

The DTI helped Tallent negotiate a £1.2 million European Investment Bank loan at the advantageous rate of 4 per cent interest. With this loan secured, further backing was negotiated through Alex Worrall's efforts from four key sources – two American, one French and one Irish. Despite the severe recession in the UK these foreign investors liked the ambitious plan and the commitment and dedication of management and the workforce.

Tallent's management realized that it was not sufficient to obtain funding for investment, but that it needed to sustain a healthy *cash flow*. This was brought into sharp focus in 1983 when, having made the investment in new technology and geared the business up with higher fixed costs to deal with increased volumes, the planned output volumes failed to materialize. The main cause of this was the relatively poor post-launch sales of Ford's new Sierra model which disappointed both Ford and Tallent. Other contracts had been won, from Rover and Jaguar, and the non-motor industry expansion continued with business from Black & Decker, Samsung, Goldstar

9

and IBM. The Ford volume was critical to Tallent's cash flow planning and bankers and lender had to be warned in 1984 that loan interest and repayment terms might prove difficult to meet. This financial crisis focused the management's attention on cash flow. As Alex Worrall explained:

Over a number of years we had become used to carrying ever-increasing levels of stock and to debtors paying late. Management was spending much of its time chasing outstanding accounts.

This pointed to an urgent need to gain better control of material flows and customer contract management.

Just-in-time and EDI

The management team recognized that the application of just-in-time (JIT) techniques was one way of easing the pressure on Tallent's cash resources and high gearing as well as providing a number of manufacturing efficiency and productivity benefits.

The application of JIT was facilitated by the appointment of Simon Flunder from Ford who was given the responsibility for purchasing and the flow of goods and inventory. It was believed that this technique would provide 'visibility' – the ability to see what was going on – and would facilitate continuous production instead of the traditional batch processing.

Alex Worrall's increasing interest in the use of electronic data interchange (EDI) provided the mechanism for realizing the JIT technique. During 1983 he became aware of the ODETTE initiative which was being introduced in the motor industry. He also recognized that EDI could bring wider and longer-term benefits than merely facilitating JIT. He envisaged a system with improved ordering and inventory control at one end and streamlined billing, accounting and electronic money collection at the other end. Furthermore this system would provide a platform for cementing relationships with key suppliers and customers.

At the same time the motor industry was changing, with manufacturers concentrating more on assembly. They were increasingly prepared to offer larger volumes to those suppliers who were prepared to invest in new processes and meet their stringent quality, delivery and price criteria. The manufacturers were also reducing the number of component suppliers in order to simplify their own processes and procedures.

Tallent's management were by now convinced that their strategy was correct. This was reinforced by the increasingly positive talk about Nissan's plans to open a factory in the north east. This strategic certainty about the future helped strengthen the management's resolve to overcome their existing production control issues.

In 1985 the company installed their EDI system which was the first PC-based system to access EDICT, Istel's system network. They pioneered the use of PCs because they did not have the funds for a mainframe. Their EDI links cost just £5000 plus 'a lot of management time!'

It is Alex Worrall's view that this was one of the best investments the company made. He states:

I don't personally believe that the company would be in business now if we had not allied the benefits of EDI to our efforts to introduce JIT.

It provided us with the critical communication links with both our customers and our major suppliers, helped us build a platform for greater co-operation in the future. It also provided us with critical, hard, reliable information.

Not all suppliers were willing to co-operate with Tallent's new system. Some, like British Steel, were not prepared to make the necessary changes for such a relatively minor customer. Tallent therefore changed their supplier to a steel stockholder who would work with the JIT system.

The better communications provided by EDI enabled them to programme up to eight deliveries of steel a day. It also provided the capability to manage the production flows through the business. This meant that as well as examining production in the traditional way by breaking down the process into small manageable sections, management could take a look at the entire process and see how 'the pieces of the jigsaw fitted together'.

The result of implementing the combination of EDI and JIT was a rapid improvement in stock-turn. Initially it improved from 6 to 14 times per annum and has since improved even further. Far less capital was therefore tied up in stocks and work-in-progress. Through EDI, cash payments were increasingly being made on the due dates which released a significant amount of management time. The overall effect was a significant improvement in cash flow.

Alex Worrall's achievements in implementing EDI were formally recognized at the 1989 EDI conference when he was presented with the award of Data Communications Manager of the Year.

Managing change

Simon Flunder's work on the improvement of Tallent's processes caused management to set themselves a series of new targets. The danger was recognized that the firm might try to change too many things too quickly. As Simon Flunder said:

You have to be careful about the degree and pace of change. Too much too quickly and the organization and its people can't, or in some cases, won't accept it. So we looked at the areas one by one. We started with 'ball-park' targets in particular areas, for example, not more than 100 tons of steel in stock at any one time. Then we'd look to see how this could be achieved and track the ramifications right through the production process. A primary objective was to synthesize purchasing and logistics as a new skill.

This objective required the development of close relationships with both suppliers and 'internal customers'.

The company adopted a *cell management* approach to facilitate the changes. Separate cells or process teams were created. Each cell was given responsibility for its own output, and in due course, for its own costs and quality. The cells were encouraged to search for ways of reducing stock, eliminating waste, improving production flows and quality. Key cell control data was displayed at central control points in the factories.

This gradual transfer of 'ownership' of production to those carrying out the work provided a more harmonious working environment as well as paying off in terms of productivity, efficiency and quality.

'Obsessed by quality'

The introduction of JIT also provided a focus for Bernard Robinson's increasing obsession about quality:

The introduction of JIT was our starting point but in seeking the required continuous production and absence of inventories we also highlighted a lot more weaknesses.

Originally we hadn't quite grasped that JIT was inseparable from quality – it isn't just a technique or a process – it's an entire new way of doing things. We found that *JIT won't work unless you build in quality*. There is precious little room for error and no allowance for rework.

He therefore stepped up training for the workforce, introduced new internal communication systems and developed a more open style of management. The 'management by walking about' style encouraged management involvement with cells and teams and promoted the entire company to 'think quality'.

Another benefit from JIT was that less space was required for stock and work-in-progress which enabled more consideration to be given to factory layout – about linking processes in a more logical fashion. Ideas from the workforce and contributions from preferred suppliers helped in this improvement process. This in turn saved even more space and enabled the process improvements to be transferred into new layouts. Gradually a true system of continuous improvement emerged.

Strategic partnerships

Another successful Japanese concept adopted by Tallent was that of 'partnering' – the setting up of strategic joint ventures and alliances with firms in the same or related supply chains. The aim is to add value to each other's operations and is in direct contrast to the 'arm's length' confrontational trading relationships that had been in vogue.

The modern UK motor industry supply chain structure now contains first- and second-tier producers, as illustrated in Figure 1.2.

The arrival of Nissan in Wearside in 1986, meant that one of the world leaders in JIT, quality and continuous improvement arrived virtually on Tallent's doorstep. Tallent's previous track record in manufacturing automotive components enabled them to become one of Nissan's first 67 approved suppliers. The company was encouraged and helped by Nissan to move towards more efficient systems and processes and also introduced to the concept of *'partnering'*. As a result of this, Tallent have become part of a highly efficient local network which conducts ordering, requisition and payment electronically, and this network now includes Tallent's main suppliers.

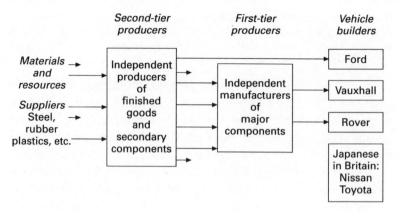

Figure 1.2 The UK motor industry – the supply chain. Source: Martyn Laycock/Tallent Engineering.

After forming strategic partnerships through first Nissan and then Ford the company was able to focus more and more on the successful manufacture of chassis/structural motor components and began to make significant improvements in profitability and cash flow. These improvements were helped by further investments in modern plant and process technology.

Tallent's first formal partnership, in 1988, was with DEA Group of Swindon – providers of precision testing equipment. Then, in 1989, they took an international step when, encouraged by Ford, they formed a partnership with AO Smith Corporation of Milwaukee, to work on the Mondeo project. This was part of Ford's initiative to follow the Japanese approach and integrate major suppliers into Ford's design and production processes.

Similarly, Nissan encouraged Tallent to create a *strategic alliance* with Yorozu Manufacturing Corporation in Japan. Under a 'technology transfer agreement' negotiated in 1990, Nissan agreed to help Tallent develop chassis/structural components for Nissan's new Euro models. By combining their expertise with that of Yorozu, backed-up by an investment of £18 million on state-of-the-art production equipment over three years, they were able to offer Nissan globally competitive production capacity.

Through a series of initiatives like manager and key worker exchange and benchmarking exercises, and exchange of technical information, Tallent has been able to benefit greatly from the partnerships.

Ownership changes

In 1989 the senior management bought out the company from Colston. But by 1992 their continuing growth had made them an attractive prospect for acquisition and they were taken over by Thyssen Unformtechnik, part of the German steel and industrial conglomerate.

The increasing value of the business is illustrated in Figure 1.3 which shows both capital expenditure and net book value.

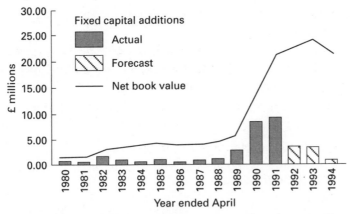

Figure 1.3 Tallent Holdings plc – capital expenditure and net book value.

Although they were now under new ownership, Bernard Robinson, now chief executive, confirmed that:

Nothing's really changed – we stick to the area of chassis/structurals that we know and strive continually to do things better. We use our partnerships and alliances to best advantage and we ensure our people receive the best training and we provide the best information to enable them to play their full parts.

The key success factors

The key factors that underpin Tallent's remarkable success include:

- *Clear leadership* from Bernard Robinson; his shop-floor background, his willingness to listen and learn and his positive, yet open, management style have had a vital influence on progress.

- Their continuing *commitment to change.*

- Their preoccupation with *improving production processes* to suit customer needs. At the same time they have maintained process flexibility – they have changed when conditions required them to – and they have adopted and adapted technology to their specific requirements.

- *Teamwork* has been encouraged through techniques like 'cell management' which has encouraged the workforce to become involved in, and to take 'ownership' of, quality.

- The use of *strategic alliances and partnerships* has both helped cement customer relationships and provided a rapid learning curve to achieving a position that is competitive by global standards.

- *Business process re-engineering* had not even been invented when Tallent's management began to streamline the company's processes, and its supply chain!

Bernard Robinson attributes their success to a number of golden rules:

Adopt a clear strategy and never ever give up.

Get the workforce working with you and never stop looking for better ways to do things.

Follow the three Ss:

Standardization: a set of clearly defined standards and objectives which everyone understands,

Specification: clear concise technical quality descriptors which reinforce the standards set, and

Simplification: make everything as down-to-earth and understandable as possible.

Tallent's achievements in the past 12 years have been remarkable. They have clearly exploited any 'window of opportunity' that became available, e.g. the timely arrival of Nissan in the area was a slice of fortune that they were able to capitalize on, and by working closely with the Department of Trade and Industry they have been able to source funds to support key investments. But, in addition to their profit growth, their success is also indicated by the fact that they created some 500 additional jobs in an area of high unemployment (see Figure 1.4).

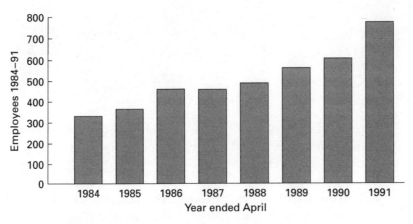

Figure 1.4 Tallent Holdings plc – employees 1984–1991.

Ultimately, like many British medium-sized high-growth companies, they became an irresistible takeover target for a larger company. In this case there was also an additional incentive as such a move allowed the managers to capitalize on their previous buy-out. This 'grow quickly and sell out' phenomenon in the UK is in direct contrast to the continental pattern where businesses tend to be run for long-term growth. But the volatile boom and bust economy in the UK and the speculative nature of business financing (e.g. through venture capital) promotes a shorter-term view.

The entertainment industry is one of Britain's 'world class' service industries. The record industry, for example, was responsible for overseas sales of £1.16 billion in 1993 and recorded a trade surplus of £571 million – as big a contribution as was made by the steel industry[1]. This chapter explores the role that high-growth mid-sized businesses have played within that industry in the period 1987–1992[2]. The entertainment industry offers a wide variety of products and services such as recorded music, radio, television, cinema and the theatre.

Profile of the British entertainment industry

Expenditure on entertainment is discretionary spending. The demand for entertainment products and services is therefore closely associated with growth in real incomes and the pro-portion of income that is spent rather than saved. Figure 2.1 shows how the onset of the recession at the end of the 1980s

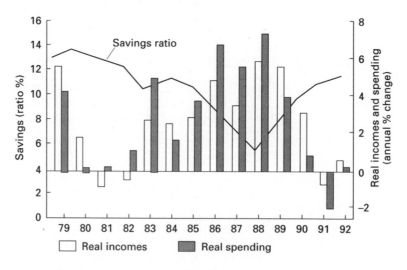

Figure 2.1 The trade cycle: real income and expenditure, and savings.
Source: CSO.

culminated in a reduction in real spending in 1991. In the entertainment industry a five-year period in which the real expenditure grew annually by an average of 3.1 per cent was followed in 1991 by a drop of 5 per cent.

UK annual expenditure on recorded music demonstrates how this type of expenditure is linked to the cycle of boom and recession. Figure 2.2 shows how annual expenditure moves around the 'average consumer expenditure' of 0.3 per cent of total spending.

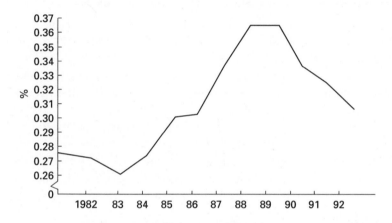

Figure 2.2 Annual spending on recorded music as a percentage of total consumer spending. Source: British Phonographic Industry.

Industry trends

The entertainment industry has undergone the same trends towards business concentration that we have seen in other industries like publishing and travel services with the absorption of small and mid-size businesses into the larger companies. The owners of the smaller business in the entertainment industry can easily become tired of coping with fluctuating consumer demand and of trying to manage creative and often mercurial artists. They are therefore often open to capitalizing on their current success when approached by larger businesses.

An analysis produced in 1992 by Inter-Company Comparisons showed how pre-tax profit margins in the film and television sector declined from 8.4 per cent in 1987/88, to 5.5 per cent in

1988/89 and then to –1.3 per cent in 1989/90. This fall in profits has resulted in the disappearance of mid-size high-growth companies in a number of entertainment industry sectors to leave the larger businesses in control. Six record companies now account for 80 per cent of UK sales, and three cinema chains (all subsidiaries of US corporations) control more than half of the total number of UK screens. Commercial television and radio have also seen consolidation of operators and ownership.

Defining and locating supergrowth businesses

In previous studies the criteria for 'supergrowth' included a minimum sales and profit growth of 20 per cent per annum over a five year period. In this case the minimum was reduced to 10 per cent in order to reflect the low GDP growth (10 per cent overall) during the 1987/88–1991/92 period. The 'mid-size' qualification was set at a sales turnover range of £10–100 million. Any company that reported a loss was excluded and only independent companies were studied.

The only sub-sectors where supergrowth companies were found were recorded music, commercial radio and theatre. No commercial, cable, or satellite television companies qualified

Table 2.1 Supergrowth businesses in the entertainment sector.

Company	Sub-sector	Size 1992 (£m)	Sales (average annual growth)	Profits (average annual growth)
Really Useful Group	Theatre	68.9	+30%	+45%
Metro Radio Group	Local radio	15.1	+30%	+19%
Boosey and Hawkes	Music and instruments	59.4	+10%	+25%
Castle Communications	Music	31.6	+43%	+13%
Apollo Leisure UK	Theatre	39.9	+24%	+20%
Stoll Moss Theatres	Theatre	65.2	+18%	+42%
Cameron MacKintosh	Theatre	22.3	+53%	+147%
Prism Leisure Corp.	Music	13.4	+23%	+18%
Broadcast Communications	Media and TV	11.2	+44%	+11%

Source: The 'Fame' database. SIC codes: 3452 Gramophone records and tapes; 9711 Film production, distribution and exhibition; 9741 Radio and TV broadcast services, theatres; 9760 Authors, composers.

(mostly because their turnovers were too large), and the cinema chains failed the independence test.

Nine qualifying companies were located through an analysis of computer databases. These are listed in Table 2.1.

Five of the nine companies agreed to participate in the study. They and the industry leaders were interviewed in order to examine the significant industry trends and the growth characteristics of the successful supergrowth companies.

Before looking at the specific results of these businesses it is necessary to examine the various industry sub-sectors to understand the underlying industry trends.

Analysis of the sub-sectors

The recorded music sector

Sales of records in the UK account for 7 per cent of world sales and total sales (trade deliveries) in the UK were worth almost £700 million in 1992. Figure 2.3 shows how the annual UK sales volume peaked in 1988 (the figures shown are at constant values based on 1992 prices).

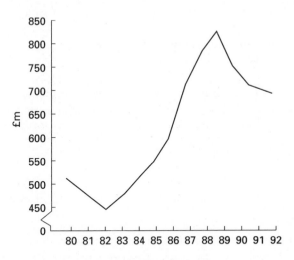

Figure 2.3 Recorded music – total UK sales 1980–1992 (constant value, 1992 prices). Source: British Phonographic Industry.

The recorded music business has been the subject of changing technology. Figure 2.4 shows that while it took 18 years for cassettes to become the dominant album format, the CD has become the preferred medium in half that time. Vinyl LPs reached their peak of 91.6 million units in 1975, but by 1992 they accounted for less than 7 million units. The singles market rose to a peak of 90 million in 1979 but it has subsequently declined by about a third.

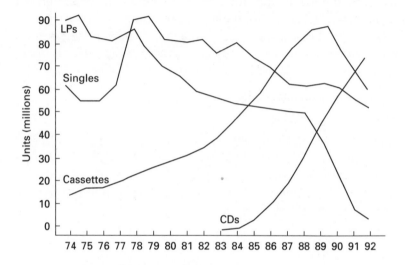

Figure 2.4 Changing technologies in recorded music over 20 years.
Source: British Phonographic Industry.

These dramatic changes in delivery technologies during the 1980s and early 1990s may yet be eclipsed by new technologies aimed at delivering music direct to the home via telephone or cables. These developments, which will also affect the film and video sub-sectors, will reduce the requirement for traditional retail shops. It remains to be seen how quickly, and to what extent these technologies will replace the current media.

Sub-sector consolidation

During the 1987-1992 period some significant changes took place in the structure of the recorded music business. The most significant event was the acquisition of the businesses of six of the highly regarded industry entrepreneurs: Richard Branson, Chris Blackwell, Chris Wright, Berry Gourdy, Herb Alpert and Gerry Moss, all of whom founded businesses in the 1960s. The consolidation process started when Sony acquired CBS for $2bn in 1988. This was followed by Polygram buying A&M, Island Records, and then later Motown. EMI bought Virgin and Chrysalis Records. In the USA, Disney financed the creation of a new record company – Hollywood Records – and set about creating organic growth.

Rupert Perry, president and chief executive of EMI Records explained the case for acquisition:

The industry's artist development success ratio is 90:10. That is, for every ten pounds invested in development, nine are lost through failure. Say I'm prepared to invest $200–250m, I stand to lose $50m a year for five years working through organic growth. Could I have bought a company for that $250m and had something there with an immediate return? With organic growth, I'm investing $250m and there are no guarantees. It's very risky.

This view from the management of a large corporation seems fairly typical; many large businesses appear to be incapable of innovation. Either they tend to be risk averse and avoid everything that cannot be proved to be a certainty, or they smother new start-ups with excessive overhead allocations and over-management so that they appear to be unprofitable.

At this stage in the industry life-cycle one would expect a new generation of entrepreneurs to be developing businesses to fill the niches that the large companies will leave as 'uneconomic' or too risky.

Commercial radio – an industry reborn

It is just over 20 years since commercial radio was first legalized in the UK. In that time the number of stations has grown from three to 130, in two main stages. In the first stage 49 stations were created and then after further legislation in 1987 a further 81 independent local radio (ILR) services were added in the subsequent six years. As the first tranche of 49 stations covered 90 per cent of the population and the next set of services more than doubled the number of stations but only added coverage of a further 6 per cent of the population, there was increased competition for both listeners and advertising revenue.

Figure 2.5 shows the development of independent local radio revenue from 1975 to 1992. Although the revenue rose rapidly from £79m in 1986 to £145m in 1989, the onset of the recession caused the growth trend to falter and the total revenue for 1992 at £141 million was lower than that for 1989.

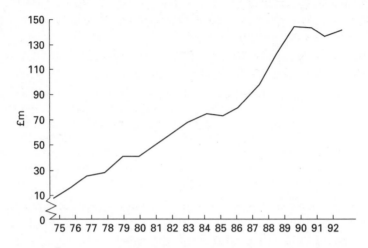

Figure 2.5 Revenue growth for independent local radio. Source: RADAD.

Many of the smaller companies were struggling and the concentration process started with the larger stations taking strategic investments and, in some cases total control, of the smaller stations. Capital Radio Group, for example, had made the following investments in the industry: 18.7% of Metro Radio Group, 4% of GWR, 3% of Clyde, 25% of First Oxfordshire, 30% of Essex and had bid for Southern Radio.

John Josephs of the Metro Radio Group suggested that it takes an audience of about 1 million to break even. The larger groups have reached the critical mass in terms of audience size and they can generate further economies of scale through pro-gramme syndication and other measures.

Radio's share of total UK advertising revenue is currently only 2 per cent, compared with 6 per cent in the USA and in Continental Europe. This suggests that there is further potential for growth, and this has been more recently demonstrated by the rapid growth of stations with carefully segmented and well-targeted audiences like that for Classic FM.

Theatre – falling attendances and rising revenues

The theatre business can be divided into the provincial and London markets, each of which have shown quite different trends as shown by Figure 2.6. In the provinces theatre attendance fell by an average of 2 per cent per annum between 1987 and 1992 although revenue rose by an average of 8 per cent per annum. In London's West End attendances held up a little better and revenue growth averaged 9 per cent over the five-year period.

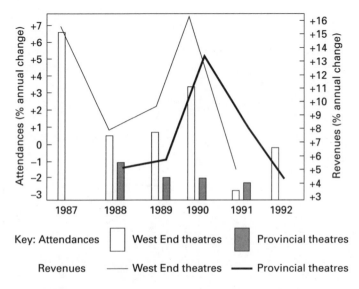

Figure 2.6 Theatre attendance and revenue growth – West End and provincial theatres. Source: SOWET.

West End theatre revenues, at just under £200m million in 1992, were more than half the UK total which was estimated to be £350 million. During the study 1987–1992 there was a good deal of consolidation in this business, with two dominant companies taking ownership of theatres (Stoll Moss Theatres and Apollo Leisure) and two leading show producers responsible for an increasing proportion of successful long-running shows (Really Useful Group and Cameron MacKintosh).

Television – stagnating revenues

The commercial television business in the UK comprises the traditional broadcast television and two emerging technologies: cable television and satellite television.

Commercial broadcast television

Total TV advertising revenue (excluding satellite TV revenue) stood at £2114m in 1992. On initial inspection this shows an annual increase of 6 per cent over the five-year study period (the corresponding total in 1987 was £1623). However if these figures are adjusted for inflation (Figure 2.7 shows the figures converted to constant 1985 prices), the average growth figure becomes a negative rate of –0.5 per cent. Thus the real growth rate of the early and mid-1980s of 9 per cent slowed down dramatically in the late eighties and early nineties putting pressure on TV company margins.

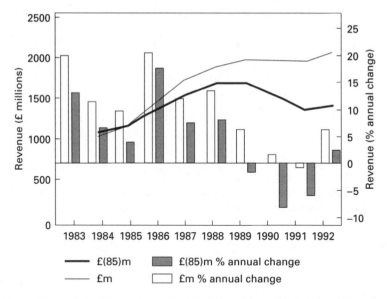

Figure 2.7 UK television advertising revenues (excluding satellite) in constant value and real terms 1982–1992. Source: The Advertising Association.

Here again the recessionary pressures combined with gradual deregulation have facilitated concentration with mergers between Carlton and Central and Granada and LWT. Industry experts expect that in the future there will be six regional television operations and a similar number of large independent production groups.

Cable and satellite television

Cable television is at a relatively early stage in the UK. The slow growth is due to the high capital outlays required to set up the networks (about £60m per franchise area), the length of time it takes to lay a cable (six to eight years for a typical area) and the relatively high price charged to consumers by the UK operators when compared with their continental counterparts. By 1992, about 1 million homes were connected to cable services out of some 4 million homes with potential access.

The merger in 1990 between the loss-making services of Sky and BSB, which resulted in the formation of BSkyB, put the overall business in a much stronger position. Pre-merger losses were running at £10 million a week and these were cut to £2 million. Advertising income has increased as the audience increased to over 3 million homes in 1992 producing a gross revenue of £423 million. Zenith Media forecast that satellite's share of total TV advertising expenditure will exceed 20 per cent by the year 2000 and be worth $6 billion.

Cinema – an industry reborn

The gradual decline in cinema admissions appeared to be irreversible in the 1970s. But in the early to mid-1980s the decline halted and an increasing trend was observed. Figure 2.8 shows this reversal in fortune, and illustrates the rise in admissions throughout the study period with admissions of 80m in 1987 growing to 103 million in 1992. At the same time the number of UK screens was increasing (from 1311 in 1987 to 1845 in 1992) and average seat capacity increased by over 11 (Source: Cinema Advertisers Association). The gross box-office revenue for 1992 was $621m representing an annual growth rate of about 20 per cent when compared with the 1987 total of $316m.

This growth was remarkable given the onset of the recession and the increased competition from 'free TV', from the continuing development of video hire and purchase outlets (video cassette recorder penetration rose from 60 to 75 per cent in the study period) and from the emerging satellite and cable TV

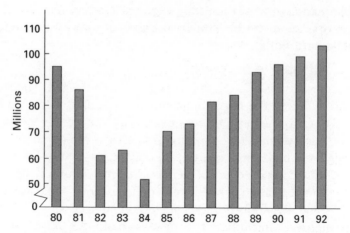

Figure 2.8 Annual UK cinema admissions 1980–1992. Source: DTI/Cinema Advertisers Association/Screen Digest.

stations. Despite the overall rise in attendance, there was an 11 per cent fall in the number of 15–24 year olds, the prime cinema-going age group.

Much of the revival is due to the growth of multiplex cinemas which have widened film viewing choice and significantly improved the level of customer service. Cinemas with five or more screens more than trebled between 1988 and 1991 (source: Screen Digest) – from 12 per cent to 37 per cent.

The three major cinema chains which account for more than half the number of screens are MGM Cinemas, Rank's Odeon Chain and United Cinemas International (co-owned by Paramount and Universal). The major distributors are United International Pictures, Warner Brothers, 20th Century Fox, Columbia/TriStar and Rank Film Distributors. They all demonstrated supergrowth qualities but all were excluded from the study because of their status as subsidiaries of larger groups.

Communacopia

The term communacopia[3] has been used to describe the new technologies expected to transform the entertainment industry. These are based on full development of digital technology potential and include the delivery of new forms of digital audio and visual entertainment direct into homes, and the introduction of interactive multimedia on CD-Roms. These essentially combine communications and computing technologies to provide new generations with a broad menu of directly accessible entertainment in the home.

The supergrowth companies in entertainment

The approach

The conclusions from our earlier studies into supergrowth businesses, as detailed in Chapter 3, were that there were nine key strategies which accounted for their success. These were:

- Early entry into growth markets
- Identifying and serving a market niche
- Diversification into related products
- Flexibility to respond to customer needs
- Close relationships with customers
- Attaching importance to people
- Attracting and retaining good people
- Having simple but effective information and control systems
- A positive leadership style

The factors most commonly associated with success were:

- Flexibility
- Diversification
- People
- Niche marketing, and
- Leadership style

Although these factors would be identified by many businesses as being critically important, the crucial difference in the winning businesses is that they pay more than lip service to these ideas – *they are fully committed to making them work.*

The supergrowth companies in the entertainment sector were ranked against a list of factors based on the success factors above but expanded to include other possible strategies. The ranking was based on the views of both industry experts and interviews with key executives in the supergrowth companies. The results of the ranking are shown in Table 2.2.

Table 2.2 Growth strategies in entertainment.

• Early entry into growth markets	✔✔
• Identifying and serving a market niche	✔✔
• Serving a local market	
• Investment in, and application of new technology	
• Introduction of a new product concept	✔✔
• Being a low cost operator/producer	
• Operating within the umbrella of a large business	
• Flexible service to customers	✔
• Exclusive design or franchise	✔✔
• Using a joint venture approach	
• Diversifying into related products	✔
• Expansion through acquisition	✔
• International expansion	✔
• Developing, motivating and retaining people	

✔✔ = Very strong response (80%+)
✔ = Strong response (60–80%)

At the same time the most important critical success factors identified were:

• Building on expertise and strengths

• Creating and serving niches

• Strong financial and operating controls

• Informality, *not* bureaucracy

When the senior executives were asked to select the most important growth strategies and rank them in order of importance the result was:

1. Identify and serve a market niche
2. Exclusivity
3. International expansion
4. Diversification into related products
5. Introduction of a new product concept

This ranking reflected the overall perspective of these executives rather than the isolated view of each parameter gained in the previous analytical exercise. What we saw here was the exploitation of a window of opportunity through either a new product or new type of niche service, the desire to have exclusivity thereby gaining market protection and the ability to develop the business further, either through international expansion or related products.

When questioned on the strengths of their competitive position, the company executives emphasized the prime importance of company reputation (or brand strength) coupled with product design and exclusivity. They expressed the view that a combination of continuing product innovation and the maintenance of high quality were vital in achieving competitive advantage.

Growth characteristics of the entertainment industry

In discussing growth strategies with executives from the entertainment supergrowth companies the importance of *exclusivity* was emphasized time and again. Exclusivity can be gained in a number of different ways; typical examples of this were: Castle's acquisition and exploitation of a 1960s' and 1970s' record catalogue, Boosey and Hawkes' acquisition of works by serious music composers, Metro Radio's successful franchise applications and radio station acquisitions, Really Useful Group's strength through Andrew Lloyd Webber's reputation, copyrights and exclusive services and Apollo's acquisition of prime theatre venues.

The strength of *company reputation* or brand value provided all these companies with a major competitive advantage. In the entertainment business companies tend to have a high profile and success breeds success; good people are attracted to a prestigious name. Where an organization is identified with a single person, employees find it easier to share their values. A classic example of this was Virgin where the personality of Richard Branson permeated the entire company. Andrew Lloyd Webber and Cameron MacKintosh provide similar leadership profiles in the industry. But not all reputations are based on the cult of the individual. At Boosey and Hawkes, for example, the reputation is based on the branded professional musical instruments produced by highly skilled craftsmen. Internally there is great pride in being close to the creative process and in being associated with the world's leading brand names. Externally the good reputation has helped build a strong market position.

The combination of *design innovation and high quality* has delivered significant competitive advantage in the industry.

Andrew Lloyd Webber's success has not simply been based on the revival of the theatrical musical as a genre, but has also incorporated the design of exclusive events, the use of innovative set design and staging, and use of a highly talented production team. Their productions have been staged with consistent and highly professional standards around the world.

Metro Radio took advantage of an exclusive franchise that provided sole commercial access to their potential audience, and built on a slogan 'More Music Metro' to create a unique reputation. They provided the programmes that the audience wanted and provided a large pool of listeners for their advertisers. By using high quality input from creative people they created innovative advertising selling techniques in what could have been considered a secondary advertising medium and this also contributed significantly to their growth.

Boosey and Hawkes' instrument division concentrated on product design, innovation and quality which built brand value which could be exploited. At the same time their extensive catalogue of high quality copyrights gave them exclusivity and a good reputation for professional musicianship. The catalogue provided them with the financial strength to withstand a turn around in the instrument division.

Apollo Leisure gained competitive strength by acquiring theatres and other entertainment outlets in key strategic positions and then investing in them using top designers to make them high quality and popular venues.

Castle Communications acquired exclusivity through investing in a unique record catalogue, and then used CD technology to re-format the titles to provide a well-packaged and highly regarded collection.

Research into high-growth companies by Siegel *et al.* (1993) found that a major distinguishing feature of high-growth companies, compared with low-growth businesses, was the higher degree of focus with a greater proportion of revenue being provided by a single product or product range. They also had a greater propensity for market and product diversification into related areas, were leaner with flatter management structures, and had developed close customer relationships. Above all, the growth was driven by entrepreneurs or entrepreneurial management teams.

The supergrowth companies in entertainment certainly conformed to Siegel's focus criteria. For example the Really Useful Group's focus has been on the shows of Andrew Lloyd Webber, Metro has concentrated on local radio in the north east and Castle's growth is based on the music of the '60s and '70s. Even in Boosey and Hawkes where there are two major divisions, the manufacture of high quality instruments for professional musicians and the publication of classical music, there is a separate and specific focus for each division.

The other criterion that was most noticeable in this sector was the presence of the entrepreneur.

The entrepreneurs

Our earlier studies of supergrowth companies had shown that the 'Thatcher entrepreneurs' were usually professional entrepreneurs, who had been trained by large organizations. At some stage, either having become stifled by the bureaucracy or having identified a unique opportunity, they had started up or bought out their own businesses. Of course there were still some entrepreneurs in the traditional mould; Alan Sugar, for example, provided a typical example of the entrepreneur in 'self-made man' mould.

In the entertainment sector, the entrepreneurs like Richard Branson or Andrew Lloyd Webber could be viewed as examples of the 'natural creative genius' running a company like a one-man band. But the reality seems more complex than this. The entrepreneurial pattern followed appears to be similar to that described by Rosabeth Moss Kantor (1983) as 'integrative' – a combination of ideas from unconnected sources and challenges to the established practices. In the entertainment industry the creative artist and the professional manager need to work side by side. The entrepreneur then takes a position between the two and combines the ability to innovate with the skill to motivate people.

The study showed that, in the entertainment industry, the entrepreneur has a major impact on success. But, in most cases, that entrepreneurial drive is not driven solely by one person, but by a professional team led by a creative individual. Thus the whole team were driven by entrepreneurial forces. A creative entrepreneur might have the ability to produce a single success but this would not qualify as a supergrowth business. It is the development of that success and the subsequent creation of a series of additional successes that provide super-growth. For this the creative entrepreneur needs an infra-structure of professional management so that aspects like professional financial management are properly dealt with.

The innovative organization

Theodore Levitt (1981) made the following observation on innovation:

Ideas are useless unless used. The proof of their value is only in their implementation. All too often, people believe that creativity auto-matically leads to innovation. It doesn't. The scarce people are the ones who have the know-how, energy, daring and staying power to implement ideas.

There are creators, imitators and innovators in the entertain-ment industry. Creativity is about having new ideas, imitating is about acquiring ideas and innovation is about putting ideas into action. Irrespective of the source of ideas, the management decision makers need to have the intuition to know what will succeed in the market place and the conviction to follow the idea through. Intuition is subjective and personal, not objective and corporate. In the entertainment industry the difference between success and failure can be slim, but failure is highly visible and public. Beyond individual intuition, reputation plays a large part – people tend to trust products from a 'good stable' – and luck may also contribute. Success in the entertainment business is often about generating more 'bouquets' than 'turkeys'.

Back in 1982, Peters and Waterman wrote about the role of 'champions' in innovating ideas. They quoted Edward Schon of MIT:

The new idea either finds a champion or dies ... No ordinary involve-ment with a new idea provides the energy required to cope with the indifference and resistance that major technological change provokes ... Champions of new inventions display persistence and courage of heroic quality.

They also emphasized the role of organizations in providing support systems so that the pioneering champions can flourish:

'No support systems, no champions. No champions, no innovations.'

The entrepreneurs who drove creativity in the entertainment businesses were also the champions. As Moss Kantor suggests:

Entrepreneurs are, above all, visionaries. They are willing to continue single-minded pursuit of a clearly articulated vision, even when the line of least effort or resistance would make it easy to give up. But they also need other people to contribute to and participate in their efforts... In an ironic sense, freedom and control, individual action and teamwork are roughly equilibrated in innovating organizations. As individuals with an entrepreneurial bent find the power tools to initiate innovation, they create and work through participating teams. And those teams make it possible for other potential entrepreneurs to step forward with useful new ideas.

The creative entrepreneur

The creative entrepreneurs in the entertainment industry display a number of characteristics which provide the platform for their company's success. The application of these elements combined with the force of professional management provides the climate for growth.

Figure 2.9 provides a model for entrepreneurial development in the entertainment industry. The internal drivers of the individual entrepreneur (boxed) are surrounded by the external drivers of professional management which foster success

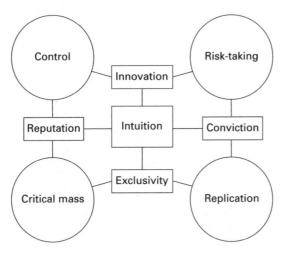

Figure 2.9 A model for entrepreneurship in the entertainment industry.

(circled). Each new product concept and market niche opportunity increases the effect of the elements and provides the further waves of success necessary to build and sustain a supergrowth company.

This combination of intuition to know what customers want and the drive to overcome the obstacles that need to be overcome when turning ideas into practical reality was present in the entrepreneurs leading these supergrowth companies. Having started the process, high quality delivery helped build reputation, and this combined with exclusivity provided the initial barriers to hold off competition. But in each case, underpinning these elements was a professional infrastructure which provided the ability to assess risks, replicate the success formula and control the commercial side. In this way, what otherwise would have been a one-off success was built into a continuing growth pattern for longer-term growth and profitability.

Notes

1 Source: British Invisibles.
2 Based on research for an article by Martin Wyn Griffith and Bernard Taylor which originally appeared in *Long Range Planning*, **27** (6), 1994. Illustrations by kind permission from Elsevier Science Ltd.
3 Richard P. Simon *et al.* (1992) *Communacopia: A Digital Communication Bounty*, New York, Goldman Sachs & Co.

Having created a large database of supergrowth companies throughout the 1980s, an important question we were able to ask was 'How did these companies fare with the onset of recession at the end of the '80s and early '90s?' It was apparent that many of the businesses had taken advantage of a 'window of opportunity' in the early '80s which they were exploiting to the full. However it was clearly going to prove difficult to sustain growth in revenue and profits at the same rate that they had been achieving, particularly when, as their businesses grew larger, the sheer volume of additional business required annually to achieve sales growth in excess of 20 per cent became significantly greater. Fast growth tends to make businesses vulnerable; for example, it stretches their financial and managerial resources. In addition, those companies growing a niche market will find that they outgrow that niche. The onset of recession at the end of the 1980s was a further obstacle to be dealt with and it would be interesting to see if the same characteristics which brought high initial growth would stand the businesses in good stead in a time of recession.

From analysing the successes and the failures a number of key conclusions have been drawn on strategies for growing and maintaining medium-sized high-growth companies through boom and recession. This chapter summarizes the main findings of the this work[1].

The first step was to determine where the main supergrowth companies identified in the earlier studies were in 1990. Figure 3.1 provides a general picture of the fate of our supergrowth company sample.

From the original sample more than 52 per cent had continued to grow profit and revenue at an average rate in excess of 20 per cent. In fact the majority of these had achieved compound growth of more than 40 per cent over the ten year period. This was a remarkable achievement given the volatility

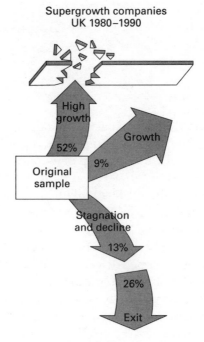

Figure 3.1 The supergrowth companies five years on. Source: Todd and Taylor, 1993.

of the economy over the period. To put this into context Sainsbury's, one of the best performing UK companies, reported 23 year performance growth figures in their 1992 accounts of 19 per cent compound for sales (£166 million to £9202 million) and 24 per cent compound for profit before tax (£4.3 million to £628 million). Some of these best mid-sized high-growth companies, which had turnover of between £10 and £100 million in 1985, had achieved sales exceeding £500 million by 1990.

A further 9 per cent had continued to grow but at a slower rate. Given the difficulty of managing sustained high growth, it is hardly surprising that a number slowed up and went into a consolidation phase. The slowing up can be triggered by some barrier like the niche running out (plus the difficulties caused by an economic down-turn), the requirement for substantial additional funding, or the need to develop the organization further in order to generate and cope with further growth. One of the problems for a high-growth business is that a headlong 'dash for growth' tends to leave the factors like the organization development and the development of new sources of funding trailing in the wake of the business – so that if a major barrier does emerge the business tends not to be in a good position to cope with it.

This brings us to the final categories of businesses from the original sample: those who have turned from high growth to stagnation and decline (13 per cent), and those which have disappeared either because the company has failed or because they have merged or been taken over (26 per cent).

The mid-size company predicament

The mid-size high-growth company is in an interesting position in which it has special advantages yet distinct disadvantages in the business world. It has broken free from the ranks of the small businesses in growing to mid size and may well have the potential to join the ranks of the larger national and international businesses.

In many ways it retains the advantages of the smaller business in not having had time to build a bureaucracy and being quick to react to opportunities and flexible in response. There tend to be fewer levels of management and employees remain 'closer to the customer' and can therefore both deliver a higher level of service and be able to act on changing customer requirements. Management can change focus quickly and communicate any change rapidly and effectively.

However, the very success of the mid-size high-growth company makes it vulnerable. As it grows, it becomes more visible to competition than when it was small and in a sheltered or uneconomic niche for a larger operator. The larger companies tend to act as 'predators' on the mid-size business for two main reasons. The first is that large companies often struggle to innovate, they are often uncomfortable with entrepreneurs who tend to be difficult to manage and control or they overload new projects with full company overheads so that they simply fail to survive. They therefore tend to 'innovate by acquisition'. A typical example of this was Derwent Foods, who launched the Phileas Fogg range of snacks. Over a ten year period this was built up into a £30 million brand, at which time it was bought by United Biscuits.

The second reason is that the large companies want to remove potential threats and acquisition of mid-size rivals both eliminates a competitor and increases market share, or provides access to a new market or market niche. One example from the sample was Underwoods, which having been built up as a chain of retail chemist shops was subsequently acquired by Boots.

Mid-size high-growth companies face another problem which is low profitability. Figure 3.2 shows the typical pattern by which profitability develops in relation to turnover.

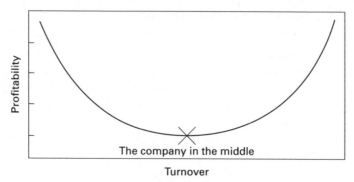

Figure 3.2 Profitability growth in relation to turnover – the problem in the middle. Source: Todd and Taylor, 1993.

The reason for this mid-size profit dip is that as the firm grows it starts to compete with large companies in the main stream and consequently suffers pressure on pricing. At the same time it is less competitive than the large companies which can buy cheaper (having more economic clout) and have economies of scale in manufacturing, marketing, research and development and so on. The company may also be pressurized by large customers, for example, the major UK supermarket chains like Tesco and Sainsbury negotiate with their smaller suppliers from a position of considerable strength. The mid-size company also tends to have to pay more for financing as it is considered to be more risky than its larger counterparts. They commonly pay four or five percentage points above the base rate. High growth companies tend to require large amounts of working capital (much more than they can generate them-selves) and do not have large cash reserves to fall back on, which means they frequently require large external borrowings. All these factors tend to act by reducing margins which in turn reduces the ability to generate cash and increases the borrowing requirement.

The increased demand for external financing by companies in the late 1980s is shown by Figure 3.3. During that period the major clearing banks were actively encouraging borrowing to fund business expansion. But by the end of the decade, when interest rates began to rise and the banks began to restrict credit, many businesses were left financially exposed.

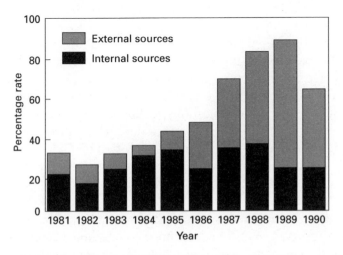

Figure 3.3 Sources of funds in British industry 1981–1990. Source: Todd and Taylor, 1993.

Given the relatively lean management structures of the companies in the sample, and the high demands on management brought about by rapid growth, there is a requirement for a high calibre of management within the business if it is going to meet the full demands placed upon it in a positive and professional way.

Despite the considerable pressures on them there are a large number of companies in the sample that have continued to grow and prosper. But almost invariably this has stemmed from professional leadership and the implementation of sound business strategies rather than from luck and personal charisma. In the remainder of the chapter we examine the factors which were commonly found in those businesses which continued to be successful.

Strategies for survival

One of the first common characteristics identified was that all of the diverse markets served by the sample companies were open to low-risk financial strategies, with low investment barriers to entry and relatively fast payback. This is a typical feature of Britain where business expansion has mostly occurred in the service industries. By comparison, in Germany, the equivalent sample contains a much higher proportion of manufacturing companies.

The companies were also in new or emerging market areas and, by pioneering the use of new technologies, competitive advantage could be achieved without a high degree of financial risk. The development and application of relatively inexpensive computing and communications technology has been particularly useful in creating new ways of conducting business which are more profitable. An example is provided by Owners Abroad plc, a chain of niche travel agencies, which grew by developing software and hardware that allowed them to compete with larger operators.

Mid-size companies in the UK do not have the financial strength to compete in high-technology markets like aerospace or pharmaceuticals which have high investment barriers.

The sheltered niche

The companies were in market niches which offered some protection against domestic or international competition. In some cases the protection is geographical, in other cases legal. For example the Net Book Agreement has, over the years, protected publishers from aggressive international competition based on a low-price strategy.

Sometimes the niche was strengthened by the development of a symbiotic relationship with a large customer. Whereas in the past a takeover might have occurred, it is now recognized that mutual interest is better served by keeping the two businesses independent. In this way the smaller business can remain innovative and flexible and not be stifled by the bureaucracy that would be applied should it be taken over by the larger concern. Examples of companies from the sample which chose to exploit their niche through the provision of high-margin premium products are Economist Newspapers and Liberty's.

Strategies for growth

In many of the businesses there was a particular event or incident which stimulated the decision to go for growth. The retirement of the founder was the stimulus in a number of businesses as the new replacement management team took up challenges that had remained dormant. In many cases the company already possessed an asset like an international brand name or an established distribution system that could be built upon.

The drive in the UK towards a market economy, which was started at the beginning of the 1980s, continued to create market opportunities as local and central governments together with public sector businesses put more services out to tender. Similarly the continuing slimming down of corporate staffs in large companies continued to create opportunities in areas like consulting, accounting, market research and facilities management.

Overcoming barriers to growth

With the majority of firms being in the service sector, one of the barriers to growth is the ability to 'productize' the service. That is, where the service is delivered by individuals, working out how the service can be delivered by others. One answer to this was franchising where the financial risk is spread but the franchisee is strongly motivated to protect the corporate image.

Access to technology

As already mentioned, this aspect was frequently the basis for the firms' competitiveness and therefore did not present a major barrier. In such firms the founder often provided the technical expertise which otherwise would be too expensive for such businesses.

Availability of trained and competent staff

All of the companies recognized the contribution made by their employees to the growth of the company. Managers were aware of the importance of recruiting and retaining high-calibre staff and had developed strategies to achieve this. Part of the strategy was concerned with remuneration, where because of the difficulty of affording high current salaries, longer-term rewards were more common such as share options and personal development programmes.

Management development presents a complex and challenging process for these businesses. A particular problem that arises is that the staff who have made important contributions in the first phase of growth may not be those best able to lead the business as it grows larger. As the business grows larger it is difficult to retain the team spirit and commitment which is apparent in pioneering businesses. Additional layers of management are put in place and the founders become more remote from both customers and employees. Managers are put in place over members of the original team and they have not shared the stresses and strains of the early days of business growth. The employees then become demotivated and claim that the company 'is not what it was'. The strategy must therefore attempt to develop the company structure in a way which replicates the small team structure and retains the flexibility and excitement of the smaller business while gradually introducing the new and additional skills required as the business evolves.

Another common barrier faced by the mid-sized company is the changing role of the founder. As the business evolves the role of the business leader changes. What may start as a largely technical, operational or selling role will gradually develop into a more managerial and administrative position. More time will be spent on strategy, company policy, dealing with human resource issues, meeting financial institutions and so on. The founder will need to examine his or her own role in order to confirm that it is developing in a positive way and is in tune with the needs of the business.

In family businesses it is often necessary to re-examine the role of family members within the business. Support from competent non-executive directors can facilitate the resolution of these issues. But it does not only apply to family businesses; those businesses led by powerful entrepreneurs can also suffer from the 'arrogance' of the leader. Having achieved a track record of success, entrepreneurs tend to believe that their instinct is infallible and the business needs strong board members who can challenge the proposals of the leader and curb the wilder ideas.

While a company is growing rapidly it is difficult to find time to stand back and examine the organization structure and skill needs coldly and dispassionately and to put in place the development programmes which will deliver future skills and competences. The successful companies in the sample used acquisition to obtain the skills, expertise and networks necessary to address their target markets. Potential acquisitions were subject to careful scrutiny, a process sometimes taking years. Acquisition deals were carefully structured in order to ensure that the skill base of the acquired company remained with the group. This was particularly important for the consultancy and marketing agency groups, where the client base often identifies with individual contacts.

Access to finance

The provision of finance is an important and continuing requirement for a high-growth business. The rate of growth puts a significant strain on financial resources. The lack of stability tends to make requirements for cash fluctuate significantly which makes short-term needs difficult to predict. At the same time the businesses do not have a long-term trading history nor do they usually have a strong asset base, which puts them in the high risk category as far as banks are concerned. This makes bank borrowing difficult and expensive.

The companies in the sample therefore were active in seeking ways of minimizing their cash requirements. Techniques employed to achieve this included:

- Using their close relationships with customers to share the risks and costs of new product development.
- Using innovative funding methods to avoid capital expenditure, such as the use of franchising to develop markets and leasing to acquire capital equipment.

- Acquisitions were funded by share issues and earn outs.
- Venture capital was used to fund longer-term debt needs with clearing banks being used to fund short-term working capital.

Unlike their counterparts in the rest of Europe, the UK clearing banks do not generally make strategic investments in business. Entrepreneurial businesses are much better understood by the venture capitalists, who historically have invested in business with a view to making a substantial capital gain typically within a five to seven year time frame.

The companies are therefore pushed towards the capital markets for long-term investment. Unfortunately, the institutional investors, who provide most of the money for the Stock Exchange, seem increasingly concerned with the short-term profitability of businesses to the point that a number of businesses have bought back their shares in order to revert to private status. These businesses wanted the freedom to develop their businesses on a longer-term basis and escape the need to justify every short-term variation to the financial analysts of the institutions. Fortunately they were the type of business that had developed to the stage that they could fund development from internally generated resources: many other businesses do not have this option.

Access to distribution channels

As the companies expanded they often needed to extend their geographical coverage to meet national or international needs. Those with a strong relationship with national retailers, for example, suppliers to Marks and Spencer, could rely on their customers' distribution channel growth. Others used a variety of innovative methods for low-cost expansion. Arrangements like 'shop in shop' allowed some retail firms to expand without the need for investment in property. Firms like the Body Shop and Kwik Fit chose the franchising method with considerable success. Franchising does offer an opportunity for good control without high capital outlay and with a controlled level of risk. The franchise package needs to be constructed in a very careful manner in order to deliver the right amount of central control while still permitting the franchisee freedom to exercise local control. A careful balance will maximize benefits to both parties.

Brand name recognition

A growing company achieves market dominance through brand name recognition but can seldom afford to do this through national media advertising. A number of entrepreneurs have achieved widespread publicity through becoming media stars. Richard Branson, Anita Roddick and Alan Sugar are among those following this path through a mixture of self-publicity, cause championing, or just by being controversial. This technique can provide valuable publicity at a fraction of the normal commercial price, but the high-profile strategy can also go wrong as bad publicity is also 'news' – as Gerald Ratner found out to the detriment of both himself and the Ratner's firm.

International expansion

The UK market is particularly vulnerable to competition. This is due to a combination of factors among which are:

- The UK government policy of creating a 'free market economy' means that foreign companies entering Britain are subject to fewer barriers (both overt and hidden) than in most countries. Britain is virtually 'a level playing field'; the remainder of Europe for example is, by and large, not.

- The standard pattern of ownership in the UK – by public shareholding – which makes companies vulnerable both through the requirement to divulge information and the relative ease of acquisition.

- As English has become the main business language, the UK is the obvious European entry point for competitors from the rest of the world, and in particular Far Eastern businesses.

This leaves many businesses no option but to be fully international and to adopt an expansion strategy rather than a purely defensive one. All of the successful companies that competed internationally did so from a dominant position in their home market. They chose to expand into the same market sectors overseas and used acquisition as the main expansion vehicle following extensive research of local market and cultural conditions. The international strategies adopted are laid out in Part 3, Chapters 11 to 14.

The 'window of opportunity'

A few of the companies in the study achieved rates of growth that were considerably in excess of the 20 per cent defined as high growth. They were not just overcoming normal barriers to growth but were typically exploiting a market 'window of opportunity'. The niche market is the natural origin for the medium-sized business. For a time it offers protection as well as opportunity. But the protection is transient. For example, if the market grows significantly, it becomes a target for the large companies. If it is protected by technical factors like patents, these expire or are superseded. The danger is that the *niche becomes a grave*. Other markets are subject to consolidation from a previously fragmented state. In these markets the opportunist maintains a lead position by moving quickly to take over or block potential rivals before they have responded to the new market conditions.

This means that at some stage the niche will disappear as the protective barriers crumble and the niche either merges with allied ones or simply is incorporated into the larger general market. This provides the opportunity for 'supergrowth' – when the company needs to grow very rapidly if it is to remain a dominant force in the new enlarged market sector. Failure to do this will often lead to the business being sold out to a larger competitor.

The process of merging and concentration is typically very fast. A number of sectors represented in the study followed this pattern, e.g. publishing, and the sector changed significantly over the period – passing through a turbulent phase and then a mature one. The concentration does not always succeed, as demonstrated by the estate agency market which was subject to a phase of large-scale consolidation and takeover followed by demerger and management buy-out as the large operators found the sector had few economies of scale and was unsuited to central management control.

The medium-sized business has to be prepared to cope with the rapid pace of change that accompanies such market movements. Results have to be delivered quickly and the organization must be structured in a way that it can expand rapidly and flexibly without loss of managerial control. The aim is to reach the critical mass necessary in the shortest possible time. Thorough knowledge of the market place is an important pre-requisite for success in achieving this but it is also necessary for the management to employ a full range of financial, selling, negotiation, motivation and other management skills to enable balanced growth.

Guidelines for success

The study demonstrates the complex, multi-faceted task of growing a medium-sized business. The task is particularly difficult in the UK, where changes in government policy, a see-saw economy and financial institutions impatient for short-term results provide little margin for error.

These factors encourage the development of service rather than manufacturing businesses, because they are intrinsically much more flexible and they require less financing – they tend not to require long-term investment in areas like R&D, technological development, or factory plant and equipment.

Progress is characterized by a process of trial and error, which enables the management to explore several areas simultaneously. The areas that show best competitive potential are then pursued and unsuccessful options closed or divested.

On the basis of their research, Ann Todd and Bernard Taylor have compiled ten guidelines for success of medium-sized businesses, shown in Table 3.1.

Table 3.1 Ten guidelines for success of medium-sized businesses. Source: Todd and Taylor, 1993.

One   *Build the core business*
Compete by offering premium-priced, high-quality products and services, in the market sector where you have significant competitive advantage.

Two   *Invest in quality, customer service and cost reduction*
Continuously invest in the business to provide a stream of new products, to improve levels of customer service and quality and to reduce costs.

Three   *Grow by 'conscious evolution'*
Set up small market bridgeheads, then 'back the winners'. Be ruthless in acknowledging mistakes and divesting or closing the misfit venture.

Four   *Diversify, step by step*

In a competitive and uncertain environment it is better to step carefully away from a known customer group and marketplace, rather than leap into a business area where the company has little experience.

Five   *Diversify into related market areas*

To reduce the risks, first build or acquire expertise before moving into a new market area.

Six   *Bring in professional management*

Recruit and develop professional managers and give them a share of the business. Introduce family members with care and only when they are proven competent and have gained the necessary experience.

Seven   *Bridle the entrepreneur*

A successful entrepreneur needs an 'alter ego' to maintain a sense of reality and to counter illusions of grandeur.

Eight   *Finance with retained profits and equity*

Maximize the use of retained profits and share capital in financing the business.

Nine   *Watch your working capital*

Be aware of straining working capital by moving into businesses with a longer payback.

Ten   *Do not over-commit your management*

Do not take on too many large projects at one time.

Notes

1 The results of this work were first reported by Ann Todd and Bernard Taylor (1993) The Baby Sharks: Strategies of Britain's Supergrowth Companies, *Long Range Planning*, **26**, April.

Part 2
How do you create success?

Part 2 provides the detailed findings from the in-depth long-term research. Chapter 4 summarizes the research approach and the summary findings. Then each of the following chapters in the section deals with a particularly significant feature in growing successful medium-sized businesses. Most of the chapters are accompanied by a case study portrait of a firm from the database.

The chapters are:

Chapter 4
Analysing growing companies - the initial study and research results.

Chapter 5
Leaders with vision - Reo Stakis
Although not all the leaders are high-profile individuals like Anita Roddick and Richard Branson, the leadership role is extremely important. As well as forming the guiding hand, the leader is usually also the source of the entrepreneurial drive for the business.

Chapter 6
Negotiating the growth barriers - Owners Abroad
The majority of small businesses remain small; what we wanted to investigate was the barriers which need to be overcome by those businesses that break through into the mid-size ranks.

Chapter 7
Critical factors for success - HunterPrint
Common factors for success have been observed by a number of business writers for various groups of businesses. This chapter examines those necessary for success in the mid-size high-growth firm.

Chapter 8

Strategies for supergrowth - Merchant Retail Group

By definition the firms included in the database grew rapidly and profitably. This chapter deals with the ways in which that growth was achieved.

Chapter 9

Growing a successful service business

The majority of mid-size high-growth companies in the UK were in the service sector. This chapter examines the particular issues relating to growing this type of business.

Chapter 10

The Germans do it differently!

The parallel studies carried out allowed a direct comparison between UK and German experiences; the marked differences observed are related in this chapter.

Analysing growing companies – the initial study and research results

The companies in context

In order to study mid-size high-growth companies, it is necessary to understand their context within the general growth pattern of companies. By definition mid-size high-growth companies are dynamic – most have recently been small businesses and have a growth rate that takes them to large company status within a relatively short time providing they remain independent. During the studies significant differences between the typical small, mid-size and larger business have become apparent and the particular and separate characteristics of the mid-size business have emerged. The aim of the study has been to examine the mid-size high-growth sector in detail using the kind of characteristics used in the model in order to pinpoint the major features that are present in the successful businesses, and the way in which they overcome the obstacles to growth in their own particular circumstances.

The study approach

The research was first initiated on the premise that mid-size high-growth companies make an important contribution to a dynamic economy. Successful mid-size companies are not only important in their potential as future large corporations or corporate subsidiaries, they also make a valuable contribution in their own right. It was also an attempt to mirror an analysis of high-growth mid-size companies which was published by Clifford and Cavanagh. *It has been estimated that in the USA whilst their 15 000 medium-sized high growth businesses represent less than 1 per cent of all businesses, they generate a quarter of all sales and employ about a fifth of all private sector labour.*

The aims of the initial study, which was sponsored by the Anglo-German Foundation, were:

- To identify high performers in the medium size sector.
- To compare these high performers with their counterparts in West Germany.

- To discover how they managed to survive and prosper.
- To investigate their competitive strategies and leadership styles.

The basic questions that we were interested in answering were as follows:

- What business are they in?
- Who owns them and how are they managed?
- Who are their leaders?
- How do they compete?
- What are their strategies for growth?
- What are their critical factors for success?
- What are the major risks for these businesses?

These types of question were pursued in detail through a long-term research progamme involving both questionnaires and personal interviews.

Defining the sample

There is no standard definition of what constitutes a medium-sized business, let alone a 'high-growth medium-sized business'. Nevertheless it was important for us to lay down a set of firm criteria in order to create a defined sample. The criteria laid down were as follows:

1. The size of the business was to be between £10 million and £100 million in 1985 (the top limit was raised to £200 million for 1990). The sample was restricted to entire businesses

2. In order to qualify, the company had to demonstrate growth in sales and profits at least 20 per cent per annum in a base five-year period.

3. A number of sectors were excluded where profits come largely from 'deals' rather than regular trading, these included property dealing, banking and financial services.

4. No companies were included that had recently suffered losses in two consecutive years in order to eliminate turnaround businesses. Nevertheless companies were included that were undergoing 'rejuvenation' and a number of well-known family businesses fell into this category.

5. Finally, the growth generated had to arise mainly from organic growth rather than by acquisition.

In the initial study, desk research of financial databases identified 179 companies that satisfied the criteria. The financial database covered the main Stock Exchange, the Unlisted Securities Market, and private companies. From this list, 47 companies were chosen as a sample for in-depth analysis. The sample was structured so that it was representative of the various types of ownership, industry sectors, company size and geographical coverage.

The research was approached both on a qualitative and quantitative basis. Each company was requested to complete a comprehensive questionnaire. This was followed up with a personal interview with the chief executive or a senior director. At the same time financial databases and press cuttings were used to provide accounting results and records of key historical events.

The research results – summary of the answers to key questions

The answer to the question *'What type of business were they in?'* was that they were primarily in services, with only 28 per cent in manufacturing. The overall results by sector are shown in Figure 4.1.

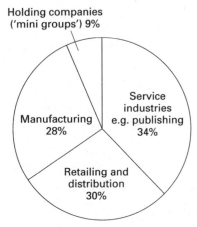

Figure 4.1 Supergrowth companies – analysis by industry sector.

We were surprised to find that although these high-growth companies were increasing their revenues by in excess of 20 per cent per annum, and indeed many were exceeding 40 per cent per annum growth, they were not operating in high-growth industry sectors like biotechnology and telecommunications. In our original sample we had included both Sinclair and Acorn Computers, which were growing at a very fast rate in a high-technology sector, but both were 'shooting stars' which grew and faded rapidly and therefore failed to meet the criteria over the full five-year term. An analysis of the companies according to the growth stage of their industry gave the breakdown shown in Table 4.1.

Table 4.1 Analysis by industry growth stage.

Emerging/embryonic	Nil
Growth	25 per cent
Mature/declining	75 per cent

Perhaps it is not surprising that there were no representatives from emerging and embryonic industries when our demanding profit criteria is considered. Companies pioneering new industries are generally required to make significant investments in human, marketing and technological resources and tend to be slow in coming to profitability, let alone exceeding our 20 per cent per annum profit growth target.

The answer to the question '*Who owns them and how are they managed?*' is shown in Figure 4.2. Although this shows a 50:50 split between family and public ownership in 1985, there were two underlying trends during the research period. The first trend was a general move from family to public ownership

		Ownership	
		Family	Public
Management	Family	15%	25%
	Professionals	35%	25%

Figure 4.2 Ownership and management of supergrowth companies.

and the second trend a move from family members managing the business towards the employment of professional management. Thus only 15 per cent were still both family-owned and family-run. The majority (60 per cent overall) were at the stage of either being family-owned but professionally-run (35 per cent) or publicly-owned but still family-run (25 per cent). Typical examples of the types of well-established family businesses that were gaining new impetus through an infusion of professional management were Blackwells and Economist Newspapers in publishing and Liberty's in fabric design and retailing.

Who are their leaders and what are their strategies for success?

There was a marked difference between the typical 'self-made' entrepreneurs found in small businesses and the leaders of these medium-sized high-growth companies. In general they could be described as *professional entrepreneurs* because many had had professional training and experience at senior level within large businesses yet had the drive and single-minded purpose of the successful entrepreneur. The common characteristics found in these successful entrepreneurs were:

- They have a 'theory of the business' – of how it succeeds.
- They provide a clear vision of the future (not always written down).
- They have 'bus-ticket' controls (key ratios for success, see page 68).
- They know how to build a team.
- They are committed to success through continuous change and innovation.

Keeping things simple and 'doing the simple things well' could be the motto of these leaders.

How do they compete successfully?

Medium-sized companies compete most successfully by deliberately aiming for areas where *barriers to entry are low*. Service businesses, for example, require low investment in capital or technological and research resources. They also try to avoid areas of strong unionization or areas highly regulated by government so that the risk of business disruption is low.

In identifying market opportunities they seek *some kind of protection*. For example, they operate in book publishing and the retail chemist sector where margins are guaranteed. Alternatively they operate in segmented or *niche markets* where they can produce brand specialities which would be uneconomical for large companies to produce or provide retailers with own label products. The aim is to avoid head-to-head competition with large competitors, or defer it until the company grows to a size when it can compete on equal terms. The medium-sized business can often compete successfully in fragmented industries that are being rationalized. In areas such as publishing and tour operation we saw medium-sized businesses competing successfully against smaller businesses by introducing economies of scale and merging with or taking over smaller competition.

By retaining the flexibility that is a characteristic of the small business, medium-sized businesses can gain a competitive edge against bigger rivals. We saw companies from our sample competing successfully in areas where *responsiveness to customers* is important – such as in the supply of fruit and vegetables to the major retailers, in the building supply trade and in Robert Horne, a company supplying paper to printers on an overnight delivery basis.

How is it possible to defend a market niche?

We were interested to know how a medium-sized firm can establish and sustain competitive advantage and build barriers to entry by others. From our sample we were able to identify a number of cases where this had been achieved:

- *The regional monopoly*, for example a brewery or supermarket having a strong local base.

- *The technological monopoly*, where for example the market is protected by product patent or author's copyright.

- *Captive supplier status*, for example suppliers to Rover cars or Marks and Spencer. There are of course risks attached to being overly dependent on one customer.

- *Sole distributor* for an importer or major manufacturer.

What are their critical factors for success?

These factors are reviewed in depth in Chapter 7. The success factors were reviewed from two perspectives:

1. From the leaders' viewpoint where they were asked to rank factors according to their own perception of relative importance. Here they were prompted by being supplied with lists of factors identified as being important in other studies (e.g. the studies in the USA).

2. From the researchers' observations of common characteristics that were present in the successful businesses.

The leaders of the sample companies identified the following 'winning performance factors' (ranked in order of importance):

1. Competing on quality rather than on price.

2. Domination of a market niche.

3. Competing only in areas of strength.

4. Having tight financial and operating controls.

5. Frequent product innovation (particularly important in manufacturing).

The results from the 47 companies which selected key factors leading to their success (nearly one third quoted more than one factor) are shown in Table 4.2.

Ta*ble* 4.2 Critical success factors.

Factor	Percentage nominating
1 Flexibility	34
2 Niche marketing	30
3 Diversification (by product and region)	30
4 People	25
5 Early entry into growth markets	10
6 More than one factor	32
7 Other	4

The main factors identified by the researchers which were additional to those listed in Table 4.2 include:

- The presence of firm and purposeful leadership with the characteristics outlined in the section on leaders above. For the outsider the most noticeable trait was the *clear philosophy for the business* expressed by the leaders. This was not always the carefully written mission statement as commonly found in American businesses; it was often not written down. Nevertheless it was known throughout the organization as the *raison d'être* of the business.

- The use of the *star-shaped organization* which essentially develops through a series of teams – project teams, product teams, business or functional teams – and avoids the traditional hierarchical structure. This type of structure offers three main benefits:
  1. It is a way of delegating total business responsibility.
  2. It offers a means of developing new business leaders.
  3. It provides organizational flexibility which enables new businesses to be nurtured and old businesses to be closed or sold with minimum impact on the remainder of the business.

What are the business risks?

These are explored in more detail later in the book. However one of the major problems for the British high-growth medium-sized business is that it is much more visible and therefore much *more vulnerable to takeover* than its continental counterparts. Financial and other corporate information is far more readily available in Britain than in Germany (in Switzerland strong data protection laws make much data capture illegal). As a much higher proportion of comparable companies in continental Europe are privately owned it is difficult to find reliable data about them. Disclosure of financial data for them seems neither so detailed and prescribed nor rigorously audited.

People came up in our conversations as a major concern for the leaders. The problem was always how do you continue to attract, recruit and retain the *right calibre of people*? Given the high growth rate of these businesses, recruitment of additional people was a constant issue, particularly given the high proportion of service businesses. They remarked that text books concentrated on the issue of maintaining products and markets and therefore had not anticipated the people issue.

Growth in these companies seems to be limited by *the ability of the top manager* to grow. Work in North America on large corporations such as Ford, Honda and General Electric shows that rapid growth is only possible when the top manager is capable of handling the growth opportunities.

It appears from our research that the medium-sized high-growth company is usually exploiting a narrow *'window of opportunity'* in a particular market niche. As the company develops the opportunity it becomes vulnerable in a number of ways. First of all the market opportunity may become big enough to be attractive to large competitors. Next, me-too competitors may introduce cheaper alternative products or services putting pressure on margins – eventually the niche may become a grave. As sales volumes to particular clients increase they may want to negotiate cheaper bulk prices. Finally the company becomes a juicy target for corporate raiders.

The main risk to these businesses appears to come from the difficulty of managing a high rate of growth. There is a danger of loss of control unless the company management constantly adjusts to the demands of increasing size, and the need to maintain close contact with both the market and the company's operations.

Who are the new leaders?

A common characteristic of British high-growth medium-sized businesses is the presence of entrepreneurial leaders. We expected to find the type of entrepreneurs normally associated with small businesses: self-made men, inventors and immigrants from Eastern Europe and from developing countries. But these types did not predominate as leaders in such companies; they were very much in the minority. The majority were what we described as *professional entrepreneurs*.

The professional entrepreneur was often a direct product of the early 1980s' recession. Before the recession there had been a long period of stability in business and most managers were content to enjoy the security afforded by a career spent in one firm. The recession then caused the contraction of many industries from which emerged large numbers of professionally qualified individuals who were seeking new business opportunities. These were ready and available to fill the key roles in these emerging mid-sized companies.

The climate of uncertainty caused many of those still employed to realize that the 'job for life' was for many a thing of the past and that they would be better off controlling their own destiny. A new breed of potential entrepreneurs therefore emerged who viewed employment by a large company as a means of gaining experience and knowledge prior to seeking entrepreneurial roles in smaller firms or even starting their own businesses.

Of course not all individuals can make the transition between being a professional manager and operating successfully as a professional entrepreneur. There are several important differences between the respective roles of which probably the most important is calculated risk taking. The entrepreneur almost invariably has to take risks, particularly when rapid growth is required. Business managers tend not to be exposed to the same extent.

Characteristics of the 'professional entrepreneur'

We found that the key characteristics of these 'professional entrepreneurs' were as follows:

1. They were *professionally trained,* usually in a large multinational company.
2. They have a *'theory of the business'* – a recipe for business success.
3. They can provide a *clear vision of the future* for the business, but their vision is seldom expressed on paper as a formal mission statement.
4. They maintain *'bus ticket' controls* – key management ratios which allow them quickly to check the health of the business.
5. They are committed to *success through continuous change and innovation.*
6. They *understand their market* and have a strong desire to grow the business and compete successfully.
7. They are *totally dedicated* and identify closely with the business.
8. They have a strong commitment to the people in the organization and tend to *operate a 'star-shaped' organization,* i.e. a small headquarters group which operates through autonomous business teams (see Figure 5.1).

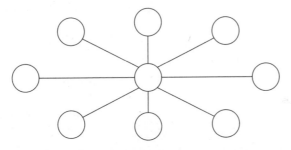

Figure 5.1 The star-shaped organization. Source: Taylor *et al.,* 1987.

Characteristics such as dedication to and identification with the business and the desire to grow the company and compete successfully are the classical hallmarks of the entrepreneur. It is

63

other characteristics such as the maintenance of *bus-ticket controls* that separate the entrepreneur in the small business from the one who is capable of developing and controlling the high-growth medium-sized business with its greater complexity. In the following section we examine some of these characteristics in more detail.

The professional entrepreneurs – who are they?

There appeared to be a distinct difference between the entrepreneur who can manage a small business and the professional entrepreneur needed for the high-growth mid-size business. The difference is accounted for by an additional measure of skill, experience and professionalism that enables more complex business issues to be dealt with.

A typical entrepreneur in this mould is Keith Barker, chairman of Videcom, a company based in Henley-on-Thames which produces terminals for airline passenger systems. Keith was formerly a senior executive both in Ferranti and in Honeywell where he designed custom-made terminals for airlines. He says he 'saw the light' one Sunday evening in a bare hotel room in East Kilbride in Scotland. He said to himself, 'What am I doing here in Scotland, away from my family? Why don't I set up my own business and work for myself in the sunny south?' So he did!

Bill Cross, founder of Brent Chemicals International of Iver, Buckinghamshire provides another example. Bill was European marketing director for Diversey, the US-based speciality chemical company. He had been expecting to be offered the job of managing director. When he didn't get it he conceived the idea of building a company comprised of small speciality chemical businesses by purchasing speciality operations from Dow, Union Carbide, and other major corporations. The corporations were glad to divest themselves of these non-core businesses for a number of reasons. For example, in most cases they absorbed a disproportionate amount of management time for their contribution. Some were too small to be economic within the corporate overhead structure and others were just too specialized.

Bill Cross talked the idea over with a stockbroker friend and there and then wrote down the company philosophy, its objectives and its key ratios. The business flourished as long as it stayed within his guidelines. When it deviated they had problems.

Although this type of person was widespread in our sample companies we also met some traditional entrepreneurs like the chairman and managing director of one of Britain's largest wholesale distributors, a self-made man who had started his working life as a coal miner.

The 'theory of the business'

As Peter Drucker (1985) has written:

Every one of the great business builders we know of – from the Medici to the founders of the Bank of England down to Thomas Watson in our days – had a definite idea, a clear 'theory of the business' which informed his actions and decisions. Indeed a clear simple and penetrating 'theory of the business' rather than 'intuition' characterizes the truly successful entrepreneur, the man who not only amasses a large fortune, but who builds an organization that can endure and grow long after he has gone.

Having a theory for the business is one of those basic management tasks that ought to be simple and straightforward. However, the task of stating the business idea has been the cause of much heart-searching and controversy in many major corporations. It is important to have this company philosophy worked out as it forms the basis for developing the business and underpins the strategy development process. Although Peters and Waterman (1982) identified the ability to 'stick to the knitting' as a key factor for corporate success, it is necessary to start by defining the 'knitting' – *you have to fully understand what business you are in.*

In most larger corporations, and in mid-size businesses in the USA, the company philosophy is usually written down as a mission statement. But the responses to the question asked of our sample of supergrowth businesses 'Does your company have a written strategy?' produced a varied response.

Sixty-two per cent of the respondents admitted that that they had no written strategy in their company against the 38 per cent who replied in the affirmative. However, most of those without a written strategy did have a very clear idea about where they were and where they were going as a business. In other words they did have a clear 'theory of the business' – what they do best and why they are successful. This theory of the business was invariably quoted by the leader in interviews and was often encapsulated in some simple phrase which was widely known throughout the business.

The managing director of one of our sample firms believed that strategy was the key factor which had enabled his company to achieve profitable growth. He said:

> We have a clear view of where we are going. Our real growth has been a confirmation of the last four years of planning ... to promote ourselves as a retail service business in the high street.

The managing director of a publishing firm said:

> Our philosophy is to keep concentrating on what we are good at and get rid of what we are bad at. The keynote is consistency: maintaining and exploiting our strengths as an author-based company; making the most of acquisitions to gain new authors; keeping abreast of, and developing, new technologies; improving service areas such as data processing, warehousing and control to keep pace with changing business and market requirements; and building a strong management team and a well-trained, motivated staff. *Given a few control figures, I can keep tabs on the 'throb' of our businesses*, including turnover and returns on turnover.

Leaders of many of the businesses, in addition to having 'a theory of the business', also expressed a *simple and coherent 'vision of the future'*. This is, in many ways, a logical development from having a theory of the business, but still needs to be formulated and then to be communicated throughout the business.

Commitment to change and innovation

One of the ways in which a mid-size company can compete with larger competitors is by being 'fast on its feet'. This type of fast-growing business remains unencumbered by the many levels of bureaucracy that limit speed of response in large organizations and which tend to make them over-cautious and 'risk-averse'.

The leaders within the service sector businesses, which predominated in our sample, were more concerned with introducing new services, creating new markets and developing staff resources, rather than introducing new technology. But they recognized that the ability to successfully manage change on a continuing basis was a major task for their businesses.

Richard Foster, in *Innovation: The Attacker's Advantage* (1986) states that successful companies:

... believe that innovation is inevitable and manageable. They believe that managing innovation is the key to sustaining high levels of performance for their shareholders. They assume that the innovators, the attackers, will ultimately have the advantage, and they seek to be among the attackers, while not relinquishing the benefits of the present business which they actively defend. They know they will face problems and go through hard times, but they are prepared to weather them. They assume that as risky as innovation is, not innovating is even riskier.

One firm in our sample, involved in the design, development and manufacture of electronic control systems, has commercial innovation as a corporate philosophy. The chairman stated:

By 1971 we had recognized the need to diversify. Although the world temperature control market was growing steadily, it had become evident that this single product area was unlikely to give us the opportunity to expand the business in the way we intended.

The following guidelines for diversification were decided upon:

1. Stay within the large but growing field of industrial and scientific electronics, as we were more likely to be successful in a field we knew.
2. Turn to areas where the market was established and the competition diverse and successful, but in which we thought we could make better products and give better service.
3. Choose products where sales in the country of origin could provide the base from which larger overseas sales could be developed.

This philosophy led to the creation and development of three new stand-alone ventures.

In a similar vein the managing director of an office and industrial cleaning service said:

Our business philosophy is to say 'yes we can'. The next morning I wake up and wonder how the hell we're going to do it. Let me tell you a story. I once walked into a private hospital in Birmingham and after seeing what went on, I wondered how their cleaning, maintenance and laundry services could be made more efficient. From these observations our latest subsidiary was born.

'Bus-ticket' controls

It is one thing to have a theory of the business, but it is quite another to be able to manage the business in a way that puts the theory into practice. In order to achieve this it is essential to establish and monitor the control measures which indicate whether or not the firm's performance is matching up to management expectations. The presence of simple and effective controls is particularly important in high-growth businesses which tend to be somewhat volatile and unstable. Quite small deviations from planned direction can quickly reveal significant risks or opportunities.

A characteristic of the professional entrepreneurs was *the ability to set key ratios and have them closely monitored*. The term 'bus ticket' controls reflects the conciseness of the key control reports we found which, in many cases, could literally have been put on a bus ticket.

The founder and managing director of a package holiday company, who had pioneered the 'bucket shop' concept in the early 1970s had recognized that aviation load factors were key criteria. He knew that he was in the business of 'providing holidays' but at the same time to be successful he had to fill seats.

One holding company placed great emphasis on financial and operating controls. They paid particular attention to return on capital invested, stock levels, debtors and key factors such as hotel occupancy rates. As their financial director said:

We use grass roots financial controls; that is, we monitor stock down to our usage of soap. Shrinkage is always due to stock surplus. When we sold our retail business in 1986, the purchaser had never seen such a low shrinkage level.

In many companies the controls were expressed in simple financial terms such as: 'achieving x per cent return on capital employed', or 'maximizing value for our shareholders', or 'sustaining growth in excess of 20 per cent per year'. But these were normally accompanied by other physical parameters which allowed the leaders to keep their 'fingers on the pulse' of the business.

Commitment to people

Another major difference between the small and the medium-sized firm is the greater number of people employed and the extra management task this imposes. Many small businesses are located on a single site and the owner or manager can deal with the staff directly on a day-to-day basis. Once the business starts to grow, however, the leader invariably becomes more remote from the operations of the business. In many cases additional layers of supervision and management are introduced to deal with both the increased complexity of the business and the geographic expansion of operations. The leader has then been forced to adopt an indirect style of management – managing through others – which can be a real barrier for an individual used to direct 'hands-on' management.

As the majority of firms in the sample were service based and hence particularly orientated towards their investment in people, there was a *high degree of general concern about their ability to attract, hold and motivate staff*.

This concern was not limited to those in the service sector, as was illustrated by the attitude of a manufacturing company to staff development:

At the end of the day everything here depends upon people – our recruitment policy is very important. Ideally, we would like to have our companies run with less than 300–400 people. We believe that small is beautiful. Creativity comes from a minimum of control over a structured situation. We leave them (the subsidiaries) alone, stand back and watch. Each subsidiary has a decentralized management structure and is in charge of its own destiny. We even allow our overseas subsidiaries to have products at a low price. We remember what it was like to be the overseas subsidiary of another company.

The founder of a fast-growing management consultancy said:

All the markets we operate in are growing in volume terms at about 20 per cent per annum. But the cornerstone of our strategy is that we are a people business and will always be a people business. Currently we employ 580 people, of which 50 per cent are 'prima-donna-ish'. That means we have to play father, brother, uncle and ogre to them.

An illustration of the staffing strategy needed to accompany growth was shown by a firm in the retail sector:

For employees, being patronized is a big problem in a family business. Nevertheless we tend to 'grow our own' in retail trade management. We have, in the past, trained our management in industrial relations skills. Currently we are in the process of organizing bursaries with educational institutions to develop managerial talent. It is from this pool that we hope to head-hunt our managers of the future.

In summary, there is a significant staff-management task within the high-growth businesses. The successful entrepreneurs have recognized the importance of people and have been able to set up the organizational framework to provide skilled human resources capable of supporting fast growth.

In our initial questionnaires the questions were directed towards business philosophy, business strategy, organization structure and controls. The problem of attracting, developing and holding on to staff was raised by the chief executives themselves as a major problem for a high-growth business. As one chief executive pointed out:

We are growing at a compound rate of 30 per cent per annum in sales. This means that we need to increase our staff by 20 per cent each year. On this basis we have to create our organization afresh every five years. We are continually involved in recruiting, training and motivating our staff. This is why our business objectives, strategies and controls must be clear, and easily be passed on to the next generation of staff.

Implications for leadership

The individual in charge of the medium-sized high-growth firm not only demonstrates the entrepreneurial flair that one might expect, but also shows considerable professional managerial skills. It is this latter characteristic that enables the mid-size business to break free from the pack of successful small businesses. The growth of the smaller business is naturally limited by the ability of the entrepreneur to cope with and manage the increasing size and complexity of the business. The resulting requirement for professional managerial skills is one of the natural barriers to be overcome by the small business with growth ambitions.

In many respects the difficult task is for the leader to 'let go'. We were particularly impressed with the resolve that was shown by the family businesses in transferring managerial responsibility to a professional management team after a long history of close family control (the degree of family ownership is illustrated in Figure 4.2, page 56).

As the company grows the owner or manager has to appoint divisional executives and delegate to them the tasks of interpreting and communicating his or her business philosophy, re-creating the strategic vision and retaining control of it – strategically and financially. This means that the business ideas have to be committed to paper, or communicated effectively by word of mouth. The leader then becomes the guide and mentor to the management team.

The study suggests that these high-growth medium-sized businesses should provide a ready-made market for tailor-made management training courses, publications and consultancy programmes dealing with topics such as business strategy, management controls, organization development and staff recruitment.

Business schools, management consultants and professional associations should target the supergrowth firms as a major untapped market for management courses and consultancy. In addition, if the government wishes to encourage the development of successful high-growth businesses, they need to sponsor the development of the 'professional entrepreneur'.

We were surprised that the majority of the firms were led by professionally trained entrepreneurs from large businesses. From this we conclude that *Britain has a large pool of potential entrepreneurs in its large corporations.* The management of these corporations can capitalize on these latent skills by either providing opportunities within the business (opportunities for the 'intrapreneur') or set up venture groups, management buy-outs, spin-offs and similar opportunities outside the core business of the company.

It is encouraging to note that many young managers in business now see their training in a large company as a stepping stone to running their own business, rather than as the first step in a lifetime career within a single company.

The problem of the 'marooned chief executive'

A central problem for the high-growth medium-sized business is *'How to continuously develop the chairman and chief executive?'* In a rapidly expanding business which is diversifying into new products, new technologies and new markets, including perhaps overseas markets, even the most energetic founder-manager can quickly lose touch with business operations. Such people chair the discussions and meet the senior managers regularly, but increasingly, they find that their decisions and perceptions are based on out-dated experience which may no longer be relevant.

The chief executives we met were aware of this problem. They were continuously developing themselves. In some cases they had been recruited to replace a chief executive who had lost touch with the business. Keeping up with a fast-growing company is a demanding job which requires a person in his or her prime, who accepts the need for continuous change and innovation. There appears to be a need for 'tutors' who will act as counsellors to these top managers. They could take the form of non-executive directors, management consultants or academics. Also there is a need for newsletters, special reports and briefings which review important changes in products, markets, technology and management for the benefit of these extremely busy people.

In due course the current leaders will need to move over to allow another younger manager to take over. At this point they may decide to become a consultant to the company themselves and to continue working on new products and new ventures. Alternatively they may wish to set up another new business of their own. Here again there is an opportunity for management consultants and financial institutions – especially venture capitalists – to help the entrepreneurs in finding a new role and a new career when their original business becomes too big or too complex for them to control.

The Reo Stakis case – when leadership loses focus

Introduction

Reo Stakis founded the firm that was to become Stakis plc in 1947. The firm grew on the concept of developing a chain of high quality, reasonably priced hotels based in Scotland. There was early recognition of the role of training staff in order to deliver above average standards of customer care. With a clear founder's vision and a well established geographical niche, the company demonstrated a long and impressive record of growth and profitability. In 1972 the company went public although it continued to be run by the founder. In the original study base period, the five years from 1981 to 1985, the company's turnover grew from £63.4 million to £133 million and its pre-tax profit from £3.9 million to £10.2 million. Following this period of rapid growth the annual sales revenue declined although profitability continued to improve for another five years (see Figure 5.2).

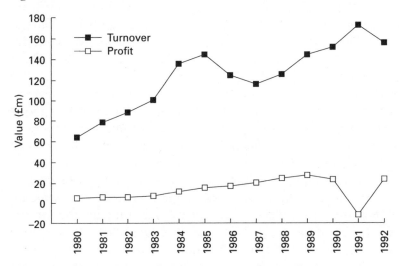

Figure 5.2 Stakis plc – sales revenue and profit development.

Diversification in the early to mid-1980s

By 1983 the company consisted of three divisions; the core business of hotels and inns, a casinos division, and Haddows (a wine and spirits company with a chain of 103 off-licences). The company was still largely based in Scotland although a programme of geographical expansion had begun.

The hotel and inns division also contained related businesses like a wholesale butcher, a plant and equipment leasing operation, a property management and maintenance business, a golf course and a time-share development.

In 1985 the company decided to turn both property management and leasing activities into separate divisions – the property and finance divisions. The growth in the financial services industry was seen as a particularly good opportunity and the finance division was to become a full provider of financial services. The group acquired a 51 per cent share in an Isle of Man company operating under a full banking licence specializing in investment banking, funds management, personal financial and tax planning services.

Although the Haddows division was disposed of in 1986, the company continued to invest in all other fronts during 1986 and 1987. Further acquisitions were made in the finance division and the freeholds of 12 hotels, previously held under lease, were purchased. A revaluation of property assets in 1987 produced a surplus of £106 million which on being transferred to the revaluation reserve reduced the group's gearing and was seen as a strong justification for investment in properties.

In late 1987 and 1988 a number of significant changes occurred. Events began with the stock market crash of October 1987, which demonstrated that the optimism about opportunities in the finance division were largely unfounded, and resulted in the finance division being sold in 1988. In March 1988 the group managing director retired and he was replaced by Andros Stakis. The group was reorganized into four divisions: hotels, leisure (casinos and inns), property and healthcare. Healthcare was a new venture based on the customer care strengths of the core hotel business. Four nursing homes were acquired during 1988, and several sites acquired for future development. A number of sites were acquired in south east England and 11 new hotels were proposed south of Leicester. These hotels were to operate under the Country Court Hotel brand. The first three of these hotels were planned for opening in spring 1990. The property division was also expanding rapidly and had acquired further development sites. A plan was approved for the development of 800 houses at Springfield Farm, Glasgow.

During 1989 and 1990 expansion continued. The leisure division added four additional casinos and two new concept restaurants in 1989 and the 20 London public houses of the Firkin brand, plus the Barracuda Club (for £11.5 million) in 1990. The triennial property revaluation in 1990 showed a surplus of £45 million and the sale of three hotels and the sales and leaseback of one more yielded £44 million of which £16.8 million went to the bottom line. The healthcare division was also expanding rapidly – by 1990 it contained 13 homes (and 1000 registered beds).

But this relentless expansion was starting to stretch the managerial and financial resources of the group. In 1990 the property division was starting to suffer because of the downturn in the property market. Profits were halved, but the division claimed success in reducing exposure to the downturn by selling some of the property site portfolio while prices were still firm.

By 1991 the combined effects of the downturn in property prices and the general recession were causing financial problems. The property division went into loss, with development terminations and sales. Hotel profits were halved, although leisure and health divisions performed well. The company was suffering from high interest charges and the institutional investors became concerned about the group's operating difficulties. At the instigation of the shareholders, Sir Reo Stakis resigned as chairman in March 1991 and he was replaced by Sir Lewis Robertson (a renowned 'company doctor').

The group instituted a stringent balance sheet asset review and a provision of £46 million was taken against property values.

The new chairman stated that the group had to confront two important issues:

- the financial stress brought about by the pace of development together with the chosen methods of funding, and
- the make-up and direction of the group's senior management.

Following a review of group direction it was agreed that the business would concentrate on the hotels and healthcare divisions and most of the remaining businesses would be divested. Andros Stakis resigned as managing director and Sir Reo Stakis, now 78, was reported to be greatly upset by these events. Figure 5.2 (page 73) shows the sales and profit track over the relevant period, and demonstrates how rapidly the problems arose (although the profit had been bolstered by the various asset sales and had been heavily underpinned by rising property values).

Conclusions

The Stakis story highlights some major problems faced by leaders in high-growth business. There is no question that the leadership role becomes much harder as the business grows in size, becomes more complex and grows beyond the boundaries of the original business. The leader either needs to be capable of developing a new set of personal skills or to employ close supporting staff who are trusted to supply those skills directly. These skills include staff management skills like delegation and communication, financial skills (such as the need to deal with financial institutions) and ways of keeping an expanding operation under control.

An early indicator of leadership problems is a *lack of strategic focus* – which is especially important when the time comes for diversification. The original business vision can then become diffuse or out-dated. This case demonstrates how easy it is for a profitable business to be attracted to short-term diversification opportunities outside its core areas of expertise. Areas like financial services can appear very attractive, but they do need special management and, like most markets, are cyclical. Ultimately, in this case, the cash requirements of another diversification venture, the property division, drained group resources and forced disposal decisions on the core hotels business. The lack of a core strategy meant that expansion was being attempted on all fronts simultaneously, rather than priorities being set.

Another problem area here was that of management – compounded by the problem of *family succession* in a public company. Sir Reo Stakis intended that his son Andros should take over the leadership of the group as his successor. His son had been trained in hotel administration at Cornell University and had trained with Hilton International and then joined the company in 1981.

When Sir Reo stepped down as managing director in the mid-1970s he handed over the day-to-day running of the business to his long-time associates. Sir Reo intended that a new, strong and experienced leader would be brought in from outside prior to his son being appointed his successor. The appointment of a leader from outside was resisted and therefore was not carried out. Furthermore, when Sir Reo appointed Andros as managing director at the age of 30, John Loughray, the previous managing director, resigned and most of the established team left during the following two years.

Management control had deteriorated to such an extent by 1991 that the group was operating from five separate head offices in Glasgow. On taking over, Sir Lewis was able to reduce staff numbers by over 100 people by centralizing these operations.

Family succession is sought by most entrepreneurs, but it is often difficult to justify to shareholders and sustain when a business goes public (there have been notable exceptions – as with the Sainsbury family). Entrepreneurs themselves often find it difficult to adapt to the changing management needs as businesses grow, and are often unwilling to 'hand over the reins'. When it comes to family succession, this cannot be at the expense of a good management team.

Finally, the group hit the financial barrier. Despite its size and profit record, it did not have a *financial strategy* robust enough, or good enough relations with financial institutions, to cope with the inevitable downturns experienced in the normal business cycle.

Many of the companies who helped us with our research had grown from small beginnings. During their growth they had overcome many obstacles. Our purpose was to understand what these obstacles were and how they were overcome. We were able to isolate *eight key barriers to growth* which they had all met and overcome. We also identified *five growth competencies* which the successful companies had used to overcome these barriers.

The lessons learned during the course of our research are illustrated by the Owners Abroad case study which is featured at the end of this chapter. Owners Abroad (before it became First Choice) grew from small beginnings to be one of the top three UK holiday businesses. The Stakis case study at the end of Chapter 5, also demonstrates some success in overcoming barriers to growth as well as indicating areas where barriers can prove a problem. The two cases show that in addition to possessing sound growth strategies and competent management, firms need a management team with a thorough understanding of the business, active leadership skills and an appreciation of how to deliver quality of service.

The barriers

The chief executives and directors of the 47 companies interviewed in the initial research found that *the biggest obstacle to growth was the need to overcome the 'barriers to entry' when penetrating new markets*. One fifth of the companies found that 'establishing a reputation where they had none before' was their biggest challenge. A third quoted 'intense competition and monopoly practices' in their industry as the most significant barrier. They identified the other main barriers as:

- attracting talented managers;
- lack of managerial talent (19 per cent);

- raising funds for capital investment (15 per cent); and
- obtaining licences for planning permission (13 per cent).

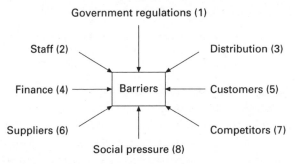

Figure 6.1 Barriers to growth for UK medium-sized high-growth businesses.

Figure 6.1 shows the eight most common barriers reported.

Overcoming the barriers

The following company experiences illustrate how a number of the companies overcame the barriers.

In public relations, Valin Pollen had built a new business quickly, 'starting from a nil-base six years ago against established and substantial competition'. Richard Pollen, the original chief executive, explained that the barriers to growth were overcome by using a strategy to 'provide an integrated, streamlined, research-based and imaginative service'. This strategy proved successful until the company made a disastrous acquisition which caused the company to fail.

Another company made a successful transition from managing a fishing fleet to providing services to North Sea oil rigs. In achieving this the company faced tough marketing problems. A drop in the demand for fish forced them out of fishing and into oil rig services. This in turn was affected by the drop in crude oil prices and consequent reductions in the demand for services to drilling and exploration platforms. They also faced increasing competition from Norwegian shippers because a recent relaxation of limited partnership rules in Norway had created tax incentives for high-income professionals – doctors and lawyers – who invest in the domestic shipping industry.

Two companies offering services to business in the industrial cleaning and security services said that their growth had been

79

constrained by increasing competition. In order to overcome this problem, each company acquired one of its competitors. In another firm, which was founded by Asian immigrants, the directors said that they had faced racial prejudice:

We had to overcome a great deal of prejudice establishing a physical presence in an industry where immigrants were considered to be outsiders.

According to their managing director, their dramatic growth was achieved through offering improved service. They expanded from being a regional-based wholesaler to a nation-wide service in warehousing and distribution. The company was then re-organized into two divisions – wholesaling and distribution. The managing director said:

We run the distribution side as a separate division. That division is motivated by profits, which is quite different, you know, from the original family business.

The growth barriers were overcome by the different companies in various ways. In many instances the companies succeeded due to the vision, guts and determination of their founders and leaders. But other factors also contributed, such as the nature of the business, the attitude and preferences of the directors, the strengths of the organization, the strengths and weaknesses of the competition and the expectations of customers. Of the many 'good management' attributes observed, we identified three as having the greatest value. These were:

• an understanding of the business

• quality of service, and

• quality of leadership.

These areas are explored before the other specific growth competences identified in the research are reviewed.

Understanding the business

It surprised us at first that few of the chief executives and directors interviewed mentioned their intimate knowledge of the business they were in. Later it became apparent that this was assumed by them to be a fundamental condition. None of them would contemplate risking their own and other people's money in ventures that were a mystery to them.

'Knowing the business' was therefore added to our list of core competences. Many of the companies we studied had strong leaders with a good understanding of the business. A director of a distribution company said to us:

When you run a business like ours, you get a feeling for it. We practise very little budgeting; up to last year there were no targets. You don't need targets in my business. Not having inventory stock or expensive machinery, we were never exposed to the downturns. We always had more money than we needed and the extra cash we had I put into short-term investments.

A similar level of self-confidence to that shown by this owner/manager was apparent in many of the entrepreneurs who had started their business from scratch and had built them into substantial enterprises.

Quality of service

Many of those interviewed stated that, 'offering a higher quality of service to the customers' was a given in the business climate of the 1980s and 1990s. Often, customer-driven and customer-focused quality reflected itself not only in the product but also in the processes and procedures adopted by these companies. A director of a distribution company explained that:

Service, quality and honesty go a long way in our business. After all we smaller distributors have had to overcome a reputation for being 'off the back of a lorry' merchants. To overcome this negative image, we rely upon quality control, keeping overheads low and stock turnover high, and responding quickly, responsibly and intelligently to service requests. I believe that's our customers' main need.

Quality of leadership

In virtually all instances the directors and chief executives had strong leadership skills and self-confidence in their abilities. One key attribute found in the leaders was the ability to groom a successor, someone who will take over from them. This is notoriously difficult for founders of a business to achieve. The Stakis plc case study illustrates how this succession process can be left too late. By contrast, the succession at Owners Abroad was managed successfully.

Successful growth competences

These are the attributes typically found in all successful high-growth businesses regardless of size. The five listed in Table 6.1

were those which were most often identified when the research interviews were carried out. They are also those which should be examined by any reader wishing to develop a high-growth business. The percentage shown against each item represents the frequency with which the competence was mentioned by the senior executives interviewed.

Table 6.1 Growth competences.

Growth competence	Percentage occurrence
Ability to diversify into new regions, markets and products	28
Cost flexibility and financial control (in particular, control of overheads)	25
Employing and retaining high-quality managers and staff	25
Image gained through public relations, marketing and past reputation	21
Ability to acquire and integrate related businesses, within a growth strategy	17

The real value of these growth competences stems from their specific application within the context of a particular business strategy and set of objectives. For this, management need a detailed understanding of the business, its environment, its challenges and its strengths and weaknesses.

It is apparent that these competences do not mirror the main barriers to growth (shown earlier in Figure 6.1). The impression gained was that companies had developed these competences as part of robust and long-term strategies designed to take the businesses through good times and bad. They provide the inherent strength for the company to overcome most barriers that materialize.

These competences are now considered in more depth.

Diversification

The ability of companies to spot and exploit new opportunities is the root of diversification in this context. The chief executive of one construction company said:

We have also moved into new areas of work, for example, in East Anglia. In the last five years, housebuilding there has been growing at a rate of 100 units per year and gradually increasing.

In this case they had taken their specialized skills and applied · them in a new region. Our research showed that diversification had to be undertaken carefully. The presence of management expertise in one sector did not automatically mean that other areas would benefit from the same expertise. For example, Stakis plc's expansion into property management was not a successful diversification whereas we saw a wholesaling green-grocer's business successfully expand its product range to include exotic fruits. In fact, diversification into areas where the company did not have core competences caused the downfall of a number of businesses.

The wholesaling greengrocer also demonstrated how an initial dependency on a few key customers could be overcome by careful diversification planning. It was important that cus-tomers with substantial marketing clout were not alienated as the company explored and developed new markets. The 'old' customers expected and received the same high quality of service as before and, in addition, were able to benefit from the new initiatives.

Cost flexibility and financial control

This competence links closely with the need to understand the business. The understanding of key financial measures provides the 'levers' to manage the business for a good financial out-come.

The chief executive of the construction company told us that:

We had to reduce overheads in real terms to make ourselves more competitive. This has meant that we have to carry out more work with the same numbers of staff.

A director of a book publishing company attributed their suc-cess to the fact that they have:

Managed to keep our overheads static year to year. The only variable cost we encounter is on distribution and book promotion.

Similar messages on careful husbanding of resources were repeated by the managers and directors of the successful busi-nesses. A director of a manufacturing company said:

We have also been particularly exposed to economic conditions. Back in 1974, for example, our major capital expenditure programme stopped. Since then we have had to batten down the barriers a number of times in order to overcome financial barriers. We might not take enough risks now because of what happened to us in the past. We are looking at a new venture, it is just a question of size. We would look at the downside risks first. That is to say we examine what we could lose rather than what we could gain.

Most of the companies had installed sophisticated computer systems to help them to manage their finances, provide good management information and facilitate budgetary control.

Quality of managers and staff

This item was emphasized time and time again by interviewees during our researches. As the companies in the research sample grew they recognized that without high-quality managerial and other staff, growth simply could not be sustained. The high quality is required because the founders needed to delegate to people who would apply the same level of attention to detail, provide unrelenting business drive, control and manage costs and deliver a high degree of customer satisfaction.

Full delegation is not always easy to achieve. The director of a distribution company admitted:

Our staff, who have been here for 20 years or more, think like me, talk like me, but don't work as hard as I do.

In this case there was a clear question mark over how long that director would continue to invest his effort in the business. At some stage the growth would be bound to tail off as those taking over responsibility were not injecting the same degree of drive into the business as the director.

Image and reputation

Entry into new markets is greatly facilitated by the presence of a good corporate brand or product reputation. It helps the business to attract top agents or distributors, and gives sales people confidence in the company's products and services. It also assists in overcoming the initial reluctance customers may have to buying from a new market entrant. As demonstrated in later chapters, image is particularly important where companies are seeking to diversify abroad and wish to use techniques like franchising to limit the investment required.

Images and reputations can be altered. A director of a publishing business said:

By keeping fixed costs down, we have been able to pump money into developing new lists in order to overcome our old-fashioned image.

In this business three of the core competences were being used in conjunction: cost control, product diversification and image.

Acquisition and integration

The director of the company established by immigrants also said that:

Later we purchased a British company to gain respectability. Now we have become a 'proper' public company.

Here we see acquisition and integration being used to create a new image.

There are a number of different approaches to acquisition. The Merchant Retail Group (which is the subject of the case study at the end of Chapter 8) focused on vertical expansion through acquisition which helped build control over the supply chain for its core business. In the case of Stakis plc, acquisitions were used to expand into related fields, but not fields in which it had the management expertise to succeed. Here there is a fine dividing line between successful diversification into related businesses and the acquisition of businesses which appear to be related but which, in reality, need a different type of management expertise.

Of course it is easy to be clever using hindsight. But there are many examples of companies following a similar road to Stakis plc. Midland Bank's purchase of Crocker; British and Commonwealth buying Atlantic Computers; Valin Pollen buying Carter; Ferranti buying ISC; TVS buying MTM have all proven to be disastrous acquisitions.

One particular disaster area seems to be the American acquisition. Because the USA has a similar market in companies to the UK, UK businesses find it easier to acquire companies in the USA than in Europe. Managers believe that because they share a 'common language' the culture is the same. It is not and entry into the American market needs the same degree of study as would be employed for a non-English speaking country.

The keys to success here are choosing suitable acquisition targets, and then integrating the acquired business properly. Ideally the integration should produce a group result which reflects a '2 + 2 = 5' position – the combined result being better than the former results of the individual businesses.

Summary

From the research work we have concluded that seven core competences help medium-sized firms to overcome the barriers to success and produce profitable growth:

- A good understanding of the business.
- Strong leadership.
- An ability to diversify in search of new opportunities.
- Careful financial and cost management.
- Recruiting and keeping good quality managers and staff.
- Building image and reputation – the latter through quality of service.
- The ability to acquire and integrate related businesses.

The Owners Abroad case which follows demonstrates all of these competences in practice.

The Owners Abroad case – overcoming the growth barriers

Owners Abroad presents a classic case of a business which outgrows its original niche market and expands into the large general market by the successful exploitation of a window of opportunity. The 'window of opportunity' means that for a period of time in a particular area the commercial barriers are low – a typical opportunity for the entrepreneur who is usually faster off the mark and more flexible than a large corporation. In direct contrast to the Stakis case, this study shows how attention to the growth barriers allows a business to minimize or avoid them. The firm paid close attention to the seven competencies listed in the Summary and, in particular, recognized that there were three particular growth barriers that they had paid particular attention to:

- The successful transfer of management from the original owner to a new team in the mid-1980s.

- The implementation of a rapid but well-planned diversification and acquistion strategy.
- Careful financial planning.

Business background

As its name suggests, Owners Abroad originated as a business based on providing cheap air travel for the owners of overseas properties. In effect it was an aircraft seat wholesaler dealing with a particular niche market traveller. A major opportunity arose – the 'window of opportunity' – for the firm during the mid to late 1980s as the air travel market expanded rapidly (between 1983 and 1990 it grew by 70 per cent). At the same time the market was becoming concentrated. What had been a fragmented market with some 600 UK operators changed to one in which, by 1990, three firms, including Owners Abroad, dominated (with a combined market share of 70 per cent). Owners Abroad had absorbed the Falcon, Sovereign and Tjareborg brands.

The strategy for growth

The growth strategy for the business consisted of three major elements. These were to:

1. Diversify from aircraft seat wholesaling to be a tour operator with central seat buying and management information.
2. Acquire tour operators with strong brands, quality products and good management.
3. Develop an in-house airline (Air 2000) in order to exploit the economies of scale that this would release in areas like administration and marketing.

This strategy for growth was designed and implemented by the management team which took over when the original founder of the business retired in 1986. They were aware of the need to build a fully professional team and aimed to do this by acquiring businesses with good management and keeping them. In organizational terms they decided to centralize purchasing and administration but decentralize marketing.

Financial strategy

In an industry noted for some well publicized financial disasters (e.g. that experienced by Freddie Laker), the management were keen to pursue a *safe financial strategy*. Once again this was based on three main strands:

1. By building a strong equity base – as opposed to funding through borrowings. This involved the following key steps:
   1982: membership of the Unlisted Stock Market
   1987: listing on the London Stock Exchange
   1985: rights issue (£13m)
   1990: rights issue (£17m)
   1991: rights issue (£29m)

2. Underwriting the company with reliable guarantees. By 1989 these totalled £40 million.

3. Through avoiding heavy capital commitments, e.g. by leasing aircraft.

The results

As a result of the strategy the company continued to grow rapidly in the second half of the 1980s despite the retirement of the founder in 1986. From 1985 to 1990, turnover grew from £117m to £500m and profit from £4m to £19m. By 1990 Owners Abroad was the third largest operator with a 20 per cent market share. Profit rose to £32m in 1991, but fell in the following year to £25m following heavy discounting in the marketplace – which caused the collapse of one large and several small operators.

This profitable growth made the firm an attractive acquisition target. In 1992, Airtours, the leading UK operator made a £225m takeover bid for the company. The management of Owners Abroad fought this by striking an alliance with Thomas Cook (the number two operator, which had earlier in the year been purchased by LTU of Germany). Under the alliance, Thomas Cook took a 10 per cent share in Owners Abroad and in return Owners purchased loan stock in Thomas Cook. This arrangement not only provided financial security but also provided Owners with direct access to high street retail outlets, a step taken ealier by rivals Airtours with their purchase of the Pickfords chain.

Although the action taken by the management provided a successful defence against takeover, the firm's top management were later censured by the City for the tactics that they had employed and they were forced to resign. The new management changed the group's trading name to First Choice and it remains the third major force in the UK package holiday industry.

Critical success factors	**7**

From our interviews with the directors of the 47 companies we were able to determine the critical factors commonly identified as leading to success in medium-sized high-growth businesses in the UK. There were no surprises; there was no new 'magic formula' factor outside the list supplied in our questionnaire. Although the directors had the opportunity to identify other critical factors outside our list, there was general agreement that we had supplied the relevant factors within our questionnaire (which was based on our pilot interviews).

The factors most identified with success in high-growth medium-sized British companies were:

- flexibility
- diversification
- people
- niche marketing, and
- leadership style

The combination of these factors describes a highly flexible business able to respond quickly to change and to minimize risk in a rapidly changing world. In this chapter we will define what people meant by these terms and investigate their practical implications. These same factors would be identified by many average businesses as being critically important. The crucial difference is that the winners pay more than lip service to these ideas; they are fully committed to making them work.

1 Flexibility

Our successful medium-sized businesses had a major advantage over their larger competitors because they were not handicapped by 'diseconomies of scale': heavy investments in fixed plant, a large head office, or a national network of branches. They could be flexible both in their internal operations and their approach to their customers. The period 1980–84, like the early 1990s, was one of great uncertainty, brought on by an economic slump. It was a time of decline and restructuring in Britain's traditional manufacturing industries.

Our supergrowth businesses avoided heavy fixed investments in head offices by organizing their businesses into small units which could grow or contract quickly as the need arose. This enabled them to diversify into new products and to penetrate new markets. Also, by designing flexibility into their processes and handling facilities, they were able to adapt quickly to rapidly changing markets, and to provide a speedy response to customer requests.

A director of Amstrad said:

We are market driven. We know what people want and what they are willing to pay for it. We have to respond quickly to demand. This is why we have retained a flexible company structure with *no investment in manufacturing facilities*. We engineer products with all the specifications and facilities that the market demands and delete the facilities that are only enjoyed by a minority. We are experts in the procurement of component parts and in understanding the semiconductor market. This enables us to develop products rapidly.

The chairman of a long-established construction company told us:

Our aim is to try to combine the best of the traditional crafts with modern equipment and management techniques, providing the right quality of construction at an economic cost. The flexibility of our organization with separate management teams, enables us to provide value for money for a wide range of client requirements.

A number of companies listed *'flexible service to customers'* as their most important growth strategy.

The first of these companies is an interesting case in point. The firm has been manufacturing processed foods for sale to the retail trade for over 60 years. They are a family business in which the founder stayed with the company for 60 years, his son for 46 years, and his grandson (who now runs the business) for 16 years. From its origins as a 'back of the van' supplier of meat pies, the company now operates in six regions of the UK in which it distributes fresh and chilled foods on a daily basis.

According to their managing director, the firm beats its competitors by providing service to customers. Unlike many of their competitors, they operate on Saturdays when the large super-market chains require supplies. The company prides itself in going out of its way to service the needs of individual customers. When a customer requested roast beef, which was not in their product range, they provided a sample of roast beef to meet that customer's specific needs. Then they made it a regular product line. Since then it has become a leading product. The managing director said:

One of our objectives is to give our customers better service, better quality and at a better price. We are continually trying to improve our distribution system. To this end we are installing a sophisticated computerized information system over the next two years.

For a regional distributor of bricks and other materials for the construction industry, flexible service to customers is also the key to success:

We pride ourselves on knowing our customers' requirements prior to making the initial sales contact. This requires a great deal of research by each of our eleven divisional managers. In our business, having sufficient inventory to meet regional demands is critical. There is a declining market for the company's core business. The small size of each division means that each person has to perform a variety of tasks.

One division manager still goes out and makes sales calls as he has done since joining the company five years before. He confirmed that the sales force stays in close touch with its regular customers, and also prepares lists of products to meet the specifications of prospective customers prior to making an initial sales call.

Once we have made the sale, of course, we can add value to our products by finishing them to individual customer's specifications. We give the service that our customers are looking for. We like to think that we give quality technical advice and that our back-up is exceptional.

Flexible service is a major selling point of this company and one which differentiates it in the intensely competitive building supplies distribution sector.

One area where flexibility pays off is *speed of response to customers*. Another successful regional distributor was originally set up as a wholesale buying operation in order to cut costs and speed-up delivery to high street retailers. The company was formed as a co-operative. All the profits were passed down to the shareholders, who were also the company's customers. When the co-operative first began operating, other wholesalers were not offering trade discounts. Today, other wholesalers' terms are similar, and the company differentiates itself by its ability to respond to small orders.

Traditionally service standards within many industries were set fairly low. They did not reflect the improvements possible through the use of modern communications technology. Some of our successful businesses have stolen a march on competitors by ignoring the accepted standards and offering a better service. Of course competitors can catch up, but it is often hard for competitors to match the real commitment to service evident in many firms within our sample. This is particularly true where this commitment is reinforced through a high degree of employee involvement in management, by direct reward through a shareholding, or a share in profit.

Being responsive to customers demands a flexible asset structure. In one company, for example, all the assets are leased or rented on a short-term basis. This means that the company can change its distribution arrangements quickly – its plans are not limited by owned assets.

However, in other cases, companies make substantial investments in order to create flexibility. A typical example was a manufacturing firm, operating in the slow-growth market for beds. Once again, flexible service to customers was highlighted as the key factor in their growth strategy. The managing director said: 'We fight back in the marketplace by meeting competition head-on.' This firm carries out a review of each customer's account once a quarter. They have introduced a graded discounting system based on the volume of business achieved, the quality of products ordered and the amount of after-sales 'trouble' encountered. The company has tried to tailor its pricing and discount policies to individual customer's requirements. An investment has been made in the development of a new showroom at the company's manufacturing plant. Customers are then flown in via chartered planes from all over Britain. They claim a 90 per cent 'strike rate' from customers visiting the factory. This customer-orientated approach is made possible by the development, over a ten-year period, of a vertically-integrated manufacturing process which permits a rapid change-over of the production line to accommodate special orders. Special orders have become an important element of customer service, and also high-growth profit contributors.

The company which best epitomizes the flexible approach is a distributor of building materials, which carries no inventory and owns all its assets outright. The chairman of this company based his business on his ability to provide service to his suppliers. He is the kind of man who would run a haulage company but not own the lorries. In order to help small hauliers, he rented them specially designed trailers to carry building materials. For this service the company charges £70 000 to £80 000 per year. The chairman's business philosophy is summed up in his statement: 'We try not to miss a trick.'

The company derived its uniqueness by building up a catalogue of products from all over the world. They operate a sophisticated communications system, employing private lines between some offices, so that information about product availability can be readily shared. According to the company brochure:

That kind of nationwide service cannot be matched by anyone else in the business. We aim to provide the architect and specifier with the full choice of colours and textures available, complete with technical back-up information including a comprehensive manual of special shapes.

2 Product and service diversification

In order to achieve high growth medium-sized companies must expand. This generally means either selling additional products or services to existing customers or developing new customers. Our companies were generally active in both of these areas and the directors identified *'product and service diversification'* as a key factor in their success.

Some companies pursued vertical integration and thereby added value to the service they provide to their customers, like the national food wholesaler which diversified into distribution. Others extended the range of products offered to their customers. Another firm in the food industry was continually developing new ranges such as convenience foods, additive-free foods, chilled foods and self-ripening produce. They had also diversified into distribution in order maintain their business: 'When we began supplying supermarket chains, we were forced to develop our storage and distribution facilities.'

As their distribution capacity grew, the company became a haulier of wines and spirits for other producers. This was a natural development as their vehicles were going to the same destinations – the high-street supermarkets.

A designer and retailer of high street fashion goods faced a problem during the slump in the early 1980s when the market for dress fabrics was declining. This forced them to look for alternative uses for dress fabrics. The company decided to use their design skills to find new uses for the fabrics in home furnishings, ready-to-sew skirts, handbags, books and so on. In this case, the product diversification required new marketing initiatives, and management identified design franchising as the most cost-effective means of achieving additional distribution.

All of our 'mini-conglomerates' diversified in an attempt to 'balance' the risk in their business portfolios. One of these companies defined the scope of their business as 'diversified industrial interests'. Following a long-term involvement in plantations, an acquisition in 1980 marked the company's entry into a new sector:

There was a conscious attempt by the holding company to diversify its portfolio away from politically-sensitive Far East countries as well as to broaden the company's trading base. There is a problem of perception in financial markets now because people think of us as a commodities company. It is, indeed, difficult to classify our identity, since we are listed simultaneously as an overseas trader, a holding company and a finance and land company.

The turnaround of the new subsidiary and the acquisition and integration of other new subsidiaries into their portfolio has enabled the company to achieve an annual compound growth rate of 38 per cent. Furthermore, the company is no longer as dependent as it once was on the prices of Far East commodities.

3 Attracting and holding high-quality staff

Many directors emphasized their companies' reliance upon the recruitment, development and motivation of high-quality staff.

Their belief was also commonly supported by profit-sharing schemes, open communication policies, management share option schemes, internal promotion, staff training schemes and other positive programmes aimed at maintaining good employee relations. Some companies, like the food distributor mentioned above, told us that maintaining a 'win/win relationship' with their trades unions was also critical to their success.

'Attracting and holding high quality staff' was also listed as the most important factor in the growth strategy of a leading UK printer. In order to meet their profitability improvement objective they have to capture a larger share of the quality printing market and keep their presses running at or near full capacity. This, in turn, can only be achieved if the operators of these presses are highly motivated. One way in which the company attempts to support the operators is through its open communication policy. An example of this policy in action was given by the commercial director. He quoted an incident where the managing director, during his morning tour, had received a complaint from one of the operators about the quality of the ink supply. By the same afternoon a new source of supply had been arranged. Within this company, management offices have large glass panels and an 'open-door' policy is in operation. Bureaucracy is avoided by keeping paperwork to a minimum.

A popular book publishing house keeps staff morale high through a policy of *internal promotion across functions*. For example, one of the sales directors was recently appointed editorial director of the company's trade book division. The company's managing director has worked in various capacities within publishing. He started with his present company as a publishing director and then went to work abroad. He later returned as managing director. He feels that company success is best achieved by a small team of top managers. The firm currently employs 200 people.

I know virtually all of them and am visible to them. My own feeling is that with 200 people, I can know them all and what they are doing – there are no serried ranks doing production functions.

He sees his visibility and informality as a most important contributor to his company's success. He says: 'The company cannot succeed unless people are really enjoying what they are doing.'

Alan Miles, the managing director of Associated Book Publishers (another of our successful publishers), also emphasized their focus on people. 'On the editorial side, we have to make sure we have the right people.' In order to accomplish this they had paid staff bonuses equal to 5 per cent of salaries in each of three years prior to our study. They also introduced a share option scheme as an incentive for executives.

The managing director of a company involved both in industrial and residential construction and in property development told us:

Our success depends on the ability of the management and craftsmen we employ and we have built up a fine team with the experience and drive to meet the highest standards. Our training schemes ensure that these vital ingredients are constantly available.

We have been successful by being fast on our feet and taking advantage of changing market opportunities. Our reputation, built up over the years, has given us an entry when market conditions changed (e.g. from public sector to private sector). Most important to our success is the dedication of our key people – we have people here who have worked damned hard.

In this business, the development and motivation of people is reinforced by extensive bonus and commission schemes. 'Rally the troops' sessions are held three or four times a year. 'Basically, contracting is a "people" business – we are as good as our people.'

A company which manufactures and markets garments quoted a similar reliance on people for its success:

When the business has succeeded, the success has been due to good management. When business has been bad, that has always been due to bad management. The two legs of our business have been our building up a good name as a brand, as well as our close connection with Marks and Spencer. Establishing a good name with our major customers as well as with the consumers of our products has enabled us to achieve profitable growth.

An electronics manufacturer explained how they went to great lengths to develop *product champions*:

We give the design staff – particularly the new recruits – the opportunity to go on a customer call for on-site servicing. The threat of having to get their clothes dirty reinforces the need for quality control. It inculcates the desire to design systems well in the first place.

We try to reward our employees for being innovative. We encourage them to set up a new company for a new product.

A company in the travel business attributes its success to informality and flexibility. As the chairman says:

We are a big travel company that thinks like a small one. Everyone here is on a first name basis. When I make an irrevocable decision, it lasts for 24 hours.

Our final 'people' example comes from Underwoods Cash Chemists:

We build our business on giving customers and our staff a good deal. If you look after both, you achieve profits. Our philosophy is to offer the public a wide range of products at competitive prices; to place emphasis on staff and staff quality to thereby give our customers better service; to create an exciting environment for customers – a magnet for them to come in and shop; and to sell high quality merchandise.

They believe that their success has been primarily due to the hard work, dynamism, and determination of their young, enthusiastic, highly motivated team. The company's co-founder and managing director had, from the company's inception, concentrated upon building a team of people who were bent on growing the business. He sets his own example of commitment by working from 8 a.m. to 6 p.m. each day. Commitment by retail staff was also recognized here by the award of prizes such as holidays.

Within the companies the philosophy towards staff varied considerably; some were formal and highly regulated while others were informal and very flexible. Success seems to stem from having a positive and clearly known philosophy towards employees, rather than having any one prescriptive philosophy.

4 Creating and serving market niches

This success factor is traditionally linked with medium-sized businesses which typically concentrate on serving a well-defined customer group and offering them a package of products and/or services specifically tailored to meet their needs. The exploitation of a market niche provides the growth momentum which enables some medium-sized businesses to emerge from the plethora of small businesses. At the same time, the finite size of the niche often forms a barrier to the company's growth into a large business.

Amstrad grew its revenue at an annual compound rate of 72 per cent in the five years from 1980 to 1985, and they attributed this success to being marketing led. Their focus was on the market for lower priced high-volume electronic consumer goods, and they developed their product range from components and individual products to complex systems. Although the company never uses original technology, close attention has always been paid to design and product development. Alan Sugar, the chairman, prides himself on their ability to stay 'one step ahead' of the marketplace by adding novel features to a standard item and then offering the enhanced product at an attractive price which their customers appreciate as real value for money.

This broad market niche contrasts with the approach of a clothing manufacturer who has built a business based on supplying Marks and Spencer. This family-run business does more than 90 per cent of its turnover with Marks and Spencer, the other 10 per cent going to small retail chains. Naturally a key element of their success has arisen from their ability to maintain good relations with Marks and Spencer, through maintaining very tight quality standards and close financial control. It is easy to see the vulnerability of a business serving one major customer, but it is equally easy to forget the great benefits that can accrue from a stable and growing relationship of this kind where management can concentrate on service quality and efficiency of operation without being subject to the vagaries of selling to the open marketplace.

Eurotherm International, a developer and manufacturer of industrial equipment such as temperature controls, monitors, process controls and variable speed drives, also places great emphasis on identifying and servicing niche markets.

According to the company's chairman, Dr Jack Leonard:

We are not pioneers. We don't like to be first in the market with a new product. We want to identify new companies that can specialize in marketplaces and not allow them to deviate from that specialization ... In a small company, one can see the results of work for customers within a few months. This enables us to get rapid feedback and also to maintain quality control.

Another technically-orientated company which manufactures speciality papers explains its approach to niche marketing as follows:

The distinction between being manufacturing-led – which we are not – and being marketing-led – which we are – is a cornerstone of our new identity in the market. In our product strategy we are selective rather than specialized, we seek market niches across the whole spectrum of the market rather than trying to dominate any one sector and we aim at the premium price end of our target markets.

For the wholesale distributor of fresh foods mentioned earlier, niche marketing is a fundamental part of the business. They operate in a sector with no written contracts; transactions are executed via verbal agreements. According to the company's managing director:

It is a very personal business. Clients have to have total confidence in you. There is a role for a middle-man in fresh foods. We used to think we were in the food business. Now we realize we are in distribution, that is, contract distribution. You might say that we are in the 'bespoke' distribution business. That is to say that our service is custom-made, designed, exclusive and personal. We have no interests outside the business except family. Being service-orientated, total correctness in dealing is necessary to ensure our good reputation. It was not good enough that we *were* successful – it was *how*.

Their major competitors are large distributors. Niche marketing may be the only means of survival for a small operator in an oligopolistic market.

Medium-sized companies not only operate in existing niche markets, but they commonly identify new opportunities in growth markets, and make an early entry into those markets. In the Britain of the 1980s there was a rapid growth in private sector services, as constraints were placed on public sector operations. A former building contractor's early entry into the property development market was necessitated by cuts in public spending for council house building. Diversification into property ownership was a conscious decision on the directors' part to make the company less vulnerable to downturns in the building and maintenance sectors as well exploiting a market opportunity.

Another company developed through the opportunities which became available for sub-contracted services in office and industrial cleaning and security services. Their 84 per cent annual compound revenue growth in the period 1980–84 was based upon the opening up of public sector contracts to private sector bids, and in particular those in surveillance, hospital portering and cleaning services.

A manufacturer of safety systems also benefited from the opening up of the public sector. This firm which grew at 60 per cent compound per annum while we were monitoring it, has capitalized on the dramatic expansion in the market for emergency communication systems. 'We were in the market place with a first class idea ahead of the others.' They created the market and now hold a commanding share. This was accomplished by using a nationwide sales force. Although the public sector market for their products is nearing saturation, the company is currently pursuing private sector sales through major high-street retailers, including Boots the Chemist.

Valin Pollen International, a London-based advertising, design and public relations consultancy, was another service-based operator entering into a growth market. The key factor which enabled Valin Pollen to achieve profitable growth was 'The identification and exploitation of an industry vacuum and the provision of top quality service, creativity and commitment'. From 1980 to 1984 the company's turnover increased at an annual compound rate of 217 per cent. Unfortunately, in seeking further growth, this company made a disastrous investment in the USA which caused the whole group to collapse in the early 1990s.

Their earlier growth in the UK materialized at a time when the number of top British companies employing public relations consultants doubled. Rapid market growth occurred across a broad spectrum of consultancy businesses at this time. The main reasons for growth in public relations consultancy were:

1. The recession which occurred between 1981 and 1984 caused many leading corporations to seek help in improving the cost-effectiveness in promotion and communications.

2. There was a need for more specialists (e.g. in corporate in-house communications) which individual companies cannot afford to employ on a full time basis, but whose cost can be spread by consultancies across a broad client base.

3. Advances in technology demanded an increase in communications techniques to assist in the explanation and
   interpretation of practical information as well as to support
   marketing efforts in emerging industries.

(Source: Carl Byoir & Associates, London)

However, less than a quarter of the medium-sized companies
we surveyed in Britain were operating in growth sectors in
growing markets. Only one company executive said, 'The key
factor which has enabled us to achieve profitable growth is the
fact that we are in a high-growth market.' In fact, a number of
companies achieved their success in declining markets by
managing to buck the industry trend.

5 Leadership style

The final major success factor identified in our survey was
leadership style. At the centre of the successful medium-sized
businesses we invariably found leaders who established high
standards for their organizations. They were also leaders who
gained commitment to their values, thereby generating a high
degree of personal motivation for quality service – a winning
strategy combination for this type of business.

Unlike American firms in which a written 'mission statement'
seems to be the norm, our leaders did not wave banners, nor
did they point to signs on the walls, yet a number of the
companies we visited did stress the importance of mission and
values as an organizational characteristic. At Eurotherm
International:

In any business sector we enter, it is our aim to be a world leader ...
we enjoy achieving and love to see people achieve ... we have read
In Search of Excellence and wish to model ourselves after – and to
become – the next Hewlett Packard.

At one builders' merchant the company's founder and chairman
said that his principle was the following: 'I am a great believer
in paying my bills promptly.' The company pays suppliers' bills
on the last working day of the month and puts cheques in the
first-class post at 4 p.m. that day. In their 27 years of operation
they have never missed a pay day. In a trade notorious for slow
payment and bad debts this firm is unique. The founder said,
'We get far more kudos for paying bills on time. Even on a

holiday.' He believes that this policy enables his suppliers to budget more carefully and maintain the cash flow they need to stay in business. Small suppliers get paid exactly how they want, but always on the same day.

If they are experiencing cash flow difficulties, we write out a cheque by hand and deliver it within 24 hours instead of waiting for the normal computer run. Of course this service is granted to smaller suppliers in return for higher commission.

He estimates that roughly 5 per cent of all cheques paid to suppliers are hand-written. Of course, the real benefit of this policy is in the priority service received from suppliers and the excellent name that the firm has in the industry.

An interesting aspect of the medium-sized business is that its 'star-shaped' organization (see Figure 5.1) and lack of bureaucracy facilitate the communication and affirmation of company values. The chairman of a multiple retail group said:

We merchandise each shop according to what we believe is the local need. For example we have four shops in the same road, each with different ranges of merchandise. Customers shop with us because of 'service', quality of merchandise, value, environment and convenience. You should be asking my customers this question, not me.

These factors help to develop customer and staff loyalty. Take a look at Dixons and Marks and Spencer. Like them, we think that environment is very important. We are making a large investment in our store environments now. We are currently refurbishing our stores. We also open at times most convenient to our customers. For example, in a business area we are open from 8 a.m. to 6 p.m. five days a week; in a central residential area we are open from 9 a.m. to 5.30 p.m., seven days a week.

One of the most successful areas for British business in the 1980s was in consumer electronics. One of the leading companies in this field places great emphasis on compiling statistics from their retailers as well as on scanning the marketplace for new ideas.

We have five salesmen in this company including the company's founder and chairman and the marketing director. Of course, the marketing division sells to independent retailers. They have a sales force of about 20.

The fact that top management are personally involved in selling enables them to keep a close eye on what their customers want: low prices and lots of features. Their secret is based on understanding the fashions of the fast-moving consumer electronics industry and it is not possible to do this when isolated in a boardroom.

Although successful UK firms tend to be heavily reliant upon people and characterize themselves as being market-driven, almost as many companies characterize their 'sense of mission and shared values' as 'moderately important' or 'not important' compared with American companies, which, according to Clifford and Cavanagh are very caught up with an almost evangelical notion of missions, values, business philosophies and the like. British companies are more reluctant to admit that they have 'missions'. Many of the executives we saw said that a strong sense of mission was an American business trait, not typical of British companies. None of the directors we interviewed produced a copy of his company's business philosophy or mission statement. Having said that, as outsiders, we could see that most of the companies were under strong leadership and had their own distinctive culture or style which stemmed from a clear understanding throughout the business of what the business stood for, despite the lack of a written statement of philosophy.

In this chapter we have shown how our winners, although operating in diverse industries, are commonly committed to providing flexible service to customers, diversifying their products or services, hiring and retaining skilled people, entering early into niche markets, and manage this through purposeful leadership. These companies are capable of surviving and growing against all the odds through their actions on these key factors during a period when their rate of growth itself causes them to be relatively unstable and vulnerable. The ability to adapt to change is also vital and enables firms to buck the trend when their competitors are suffering. In the words of Clifford and Cavanagh:

Such companies also anticipate changes, respond to adversity, and adapt to a changing world. In turn their strategies and their adaptiveness are products of their organizational strength – their clear sense of direction, their people, systems, values and structures. They combine competence with motivation, the skill and the will. And there are no such organizations except those created and sustained by committed, able leaders – who not only put it all together, but keep it that way.

Our companies are diverse – as are their strategies for success – but they are united in their ability to adapt quickly to changing circumstances and above all put their strategies into practice.

The HunterPrint case – failing to recognize the key success factors

Introduction

HunterPrint operated for many years as a high-growth and profitable medium-sized business within the printing industry. It achieved dominance in its niche through delivering superior levels of service which in turn were enabled by a high level of investment in printing technology. Although a public company it was managed and controlled by the founder.

1984–1987: a period of expansion

By 1984 the company had become cash rich as a result of its profitable growth and it was decided to expand into new market areas through acquisition. Two companies were acquired and major investments were made in both, in order to bring production facilities up to the level required in the group. These investments were funded internally. Sales offices were established in Sweden and Belgium and European sales grew, particularly in Germany.

By 1986 the company had been reorganized into four divisions, each division representing a particular market sector, and the management structure had been altered to suit the new divisional structure.

By 1987 investment in production facilities was continuing. Meanwhile, efforts were being made to improve sales and equipment utilization. The company had developed the idea of 'cross fertilization' whereby separate divisions would pool their expertise in order to complete complex projects for particular clients.

The company set up a joint venture with an American company in order to offer a 'real time' service on both sides of the

Atlantic. Once again heavy investment was required in order to enable this business to match group service standards.

At this time a decision was taken to combine the production facilities of the original business on a purpose built site. The intention was to provide economies of scale and levels of service matching the best competitors in Europe.

1988: growth starts to slow

The divisions, other than the original business, traded less well than planned despite the efforts made to improve results. The American joint venture was experiencing some difficulty in bringing equipment on line. The continuing investment programme could no longer be funded from cash flow and a rights issue of £10 million was made.

A high street print shop was opened and then closed within the year, fortunately the equipment purchased for this could be re-deployed elsewhere. A specialist company was acquired to add to one division. The development of the new main site continued and was absorbing much management time. The trend in financial results is shown in Figure 7.1.

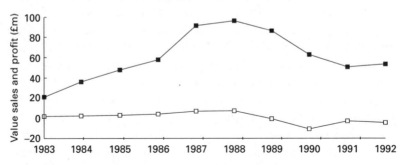

Figure 7.1 HunterPrint Group – financial results 1983–1992.

1989: failure

The large capital demands of the new site combined with late completion caused the business to run out of cash and to fail. All the divisions were finding trading difficult as the UK recession took hold. However, the main cause of the problem was a 30 per cent drop in sales in the core business as a direct result of the inability to provide proper customer service due to the disruption caused by the late opening of the new facility. The core business suffered an enormous loss which could only be partially offset by profit in other divisions.

Emergency re-organization involved the divestment of one division and re-financing was sought.

1990–1994: rescue attempts

By 1990 the founder was the only member of the management team still employed by the business. Then, under a financial rescue package supported by pension funds and other institutional investors, control of the business was transferred to a new high-profile chairman and management team. Their efforts did not ultimately prove successful and the business was again sold on. Despite several 'rescue' attempts, by 1994 no team had so far managed to put the business back onto a full commercial footing.

Main conclusions

HunterPrint showed the classic symptoms of businesses that outgrow their original entrepreneurial base and fail to recognize many of the key factors for success. It is easy to assume that the formula that works in one market (i.e. high investment in technology and high levels of service) will apply elsewhere. *High capital investment often both restricts flexibility – once you have made the investment you are stuck with it – and increases financial vulnerability.* In this case investment was made without sufficient investigation of the market's ability to pay back the investment. Similarly, in the joint venture, the company bore all the investment risk and the joint venture partner failed to deliver the promised sales volumes. *The underlying financial strategy of the group was not robust* enough to carry the group through the combined problems caused by the late delivery of the new facility and low profitability in other divisions.

The founder of the business failed to grasp the vital dependency of the firm on its core business and the diversification strategy became a weakness.

As a business grows the role of the business leader changes considerably. In the early stages the entrepreneurial style works well as it remains relatively easy to keep contact with staff, customers and suppliers and drive the business with enthusiasm.

In addition a more professional 'hands-off' approach is required where the longer-term implications of business decisions need to be thought through. At the same time the inevitable increase in remoteness of the leader from the 'coal face' means that *the leader needs to set up new information channels in order to remain in control*. If the founder of HunterPrint had appreciated the financial implications of some of the key decisions, he would either have made different decisions or been able to pre-empt the financial needs of the business. As it was, by the time the sudden onset of the financial crisis occurred it was too late to act, as the credibility of the management team had evaporated.

Strategies for supergrowth 8

Introduction

This chapter deals with two key strategic elements which contribute towards the supergrowth company: marketing entry strategies and growth strategies. It also examines the phases of growth that industries pass through and the different strategies that are appropriate to each phase. The chapter concludes with the Merchant Retail Group case study which demonstrates many of the issues faced by a management team attempting to achieve rapid and profitable growth.

When considering the first of these topics, entry strategies, it is necessary to examine the types of firms in the database. The 47 companies which made up our core research sample came from many different industries. However, the greater proportion, some two thirds, were drawn from the service sector. The remaining one third were from manufacturing and related industries. The significance of the bias towards the service sector could be attributed to a number of factors. One factor was the relatively low entry costs typically found in service markets which meant there was a small financial barrier to overcome – an important concern in a period of recession when funds are difficult to come by. Another factor was the 'window of opportunity' provided by the privatization or 'out-sourcing' of many public sector services at that time.

The relatively low financial barriers to entry in service industries mean that competition may be plentiful. The early entrant must therefore create other barriers rapidly in order to discourage rivals. This may be through offering a level of service that is difficult to emulate, or by tying up key customers with long-term contracts.

The 'window of opportunity' also featured in the analysis of growth strategies. At any particular time certain industries go through a period of rapid growth. This is not merely limited to high technology industries like computing or telecommunications, but also occurs in other industries. During our study we saw rapid growth, for example, in the publishing, travel and advertising industries. Such growth is often exploited by medium-sized companies which have the entrepreneurial attitude and flexibility to pursue the opportunities presented. The period of growth is then frequently followed by a period of consolidation when the high-growth companies are acquired by the industry giants.

The growth strategy is also affected by the growth stage of the company itself. This factor is reviewed in more depth in Chapter 15. We observed that companies themselves have to be at a point at which they can deal with the stresses and strains that accompany rapid growth. These are usually quite separate from the qualities needed to develop a small business. In this chapter we report upon the common strategies used to create rapid growth which generally fall into a number of discrete patterns.

Entry strategies

The following section deals with five types of entry strategy. As mentioned in the introduction, one common starting point was the low financial barrier to market entry. Niche markets which could be entered through a franchise or a monopoly were also common targets. Whichever strategic option was chosen, *the one common factor present in most firms was a thorough knowledge and understanding both of the product or service offered and of the target customer group.*

1 Low barriers to entry

It was found that British high-growth medium-sized companies tended to operate in the businesses which required low capital investment and low R&D investment. They were also in markets where there was a low level of government regulation, little unionization and a ready supply of labour. Service businesses can often be started with relatively little capital expenditure (as opposed to manufacturing businesses). This is particularly true of the businesses that sell people's time. These include services such as management consultancy, temporary staff agencies, security firms and so on.

This kind of entry strategy would not breed a Sony Corporation but could well foster a variety of businesses like the Body Shop.

2 Entering premium market segments

A number of companies chose to enter market niches where customers were willing to pay a premium for quality services. Examples of these were:

- High-quality, four-colour printing.
- Well-designed bathrooms and kitchens.
- High-quality laboratory papers and chromatography equipment.
- Escape systems for jet fighters.

Typically these firms used a technology or a skills barrier to justify the premium price of the service and to act as a barrier to competition.

3 Establishing a franchise or monopoly

Other companies became suppliers for much larger organizations. Having gained the supply or service contract, they kept it by providing an excellent service, e.g. manufacturing to strict customer specifications and delivering 'on time' every time. In exchange for this higher quality service they were awarded sizeable contracts at good margins.

At one time there was a phase when large businesses operated a confrontational relationship with their suppliers and kept them at arm's length. More recently there has been a trend for much more co-operation. For example, in the motor manufacturing industry medium-sized businesses like Tallent Engineering have become 'tier one' suppliers to the industry majors and as such have developed special relationships with their major customers.

The consolidation of the UK retail industry in areas like food, clothing and DIY has provided opportunities for many key suppliers. The large chains like to depend upon a limited number of suppliers who offer a cost-effective, flexible and responsive service which may include the production of private label brands. Of course, a high dependency on one or a few customers is a double-edged sword – it can leave the supplier vulnerable.

This type of entry strategy must be accompanied by management vigilance. There is no room for complacency in this type of relationship and the supplier must try to keep one step ahead of the customer.

4 Contracting out

Many companies had entered the new markets which had been created by the cutbacks imposed by the government on the public services and the 'slimming-down' of large companies' head offices during the recession of the early 1980s and thereafter. These companies, a third of the sample, were supplying business services such as office cleaning, industrial catering and refuse disposal. The firms which benefited from cutbacks in the private sector offered management consultancy, training and recruitment services and public relations. Many of the management buy-outs of public sector services, although conducted at arm's length, involved a 'back-to-back' arrangement of a contract award plus a transfer of the staff and sale of the associated assets – a formula which often resulted in the new company starting with positive cash flow from day one.

5 Packaging products or skills

Some companies bought in components or entire products from overseas, particularly from the Far East. These were 'packaged' into product offerings designed for the British market. These companies utilized low-cost assembly labour and the low-cost components originally produced in bulk for Japanese manufacturers. Amstrad was one of the most successful of these 'packaging' companies. Other high-growth companies packaged radio paging, cellular telephone systems and medical alarm systems.

These entry strategies provided the initial growth momentum for small businesses or in certain cases new start-up businesses. Having gained this initial momentum, management then required a growth strategy to take the business to the next growth stage.

Growth strategies

The growth strategies adopted by these supergrowth companies are outlined below.

1 Diversification and international expansion

Companies in the services sector diversified into new services areas, customer groups and regions, as was the case with the publishers and medium-sized contractors. Others, such as Valin Pollen sought overseas markets in an effort to remove their dependence on the UK market alone.

2 Flexibility and quick response to customer needs

Manufacturing companies depended on having flexible operations and production systems which enabled them to respond fast to changes imposed on them by special orders, changing fashions, and surges or drops in demand.

3 Innovation, introducing new products and new technologies

These companies depended on the exploitation of new technologies such as management information systems, advanced materials, robotics and such like. Underwriting these capabilities was the fact that these companies prided themselves on the reliability and quality of the service they offered.

4 Talented and highly motivated staff

A successful medium-sized manufacturer in Britain bases its strategy on finding a critical mixture of new technology and staff who can exploit these technologies and sell their products. One company chairman claimed that staffing was the most critical factor, that he was 'persistent in looking for the right men to run his operation' and that he was 'actively recruiting in the United States'.

5 Partnership with large manufacturers or large retailers

Distributors based their strategy for growth on the reputation of their suppliers and their customers. They used the reputation of their customers to gain commercial advantage from their suppliers and used the reputation of the suppliers and their products to gain access to customers. Since most distributors depend on this strategy to be credible to their suppliers and customers, their competitive advantage was gained by showing greater flexibility to special customer requirements and a faster and more reliable response to orders placed. One of the distributors said that:

Service, quality and honesty go a long way in our business. After all, we smaller distributors have had to overcome a reputation of being 'off the back of a lorry' merchants. To overcome this negative image, we rely on quality control, keeping overheads low and stock turnover high, and respond quickly, responsibly and intelligently to service requests. I believe that's our customers' main need.

6 Niche marketing

Retailers, particularly the medium-sized businesses, seemed to base their success on two factors. First, their ability to define and respond to customer needs which were specific to the area being served and, second, the expertise of their store managers not only in motivating their staff to sell the products that were stocked, but also in anticipating customer needs. One company chief executive said that, 'we merchandise each shop according to what we believe is the local need. For example, we have three shops in one street, each with a different range of merchandise.' To help them understand the market some companies used the type of research techniques that have been increasingly used by major retailers such as the in-store customer panel to get feedback about new products, store layout and presentation.

7 Financial controls

The financial controls used by these companies constitute a main factor for their success. Underwoods, a multiple retail chemist chain which was later taken over by Boots, had a monthly reporting system which enabled management to monitor all the key financial data including product line information such as sales revenue and gross margins, the main variable costs – wages and store costs – and capital expenditure. They used this information to reward their employees for superior performance, plan additional sites, and manage the inventory of 'fad' items.

8 Companies 'sticking to their knitting'

Companies tended to stay within a particular sector and within a particular industry. Retailers would not move into manufacturing and manufacturers showed no desire to go into retailing. Chief executives of service businesses deliberately shied away from capital-intensive industries. In general our interviewees stuck to the industries they best understood and avoided straying into uncharted waters. At Normans plc, a regional supermarket chain, the directors said, 'we will avoid businesses where we do not have satisfactory management skills'.

9 The search for excellence

Whilst they stuck to their knitting it seemed appropriate to also assess whether companies in different industries used similar strategies to achieve their growth. When this area was explored some interesting points of view were expressed. Underwoods, the multiple chemists said, 'We believe in *doing whatever we do, well.*' Eurotherm International plc, manufacturers of electronic instruments said, 'In any business sector we enter, it is our aim to be world leaders ... we enjoy achieving and love to see our people achieve.' 'Doing things well' really mattered in this business.

Analysis of the research database by sector provided a profile of top growth strategies. The result, shown in Table 8.1, shows a good degree of correlation between sectors.

Table 8.1 Growth strategy profile of UK supergrowth companies by industry sector.

Sector and percentage of sample (no. of firms)	*Five top strategies*				
	1	*2*	*3*	*4*	*5*
Services 34 (16)	Early market entry	Niche marketing	Flexible service	Investment/ new technology	Attract/retain key people
Manufacturing 26 (12)	Investment/ new technology	Niche marketing	Flexible service	Attract/retain key people	Diversification
Distribution 21 (10)	Niche marketing	Flexible service	Diversification	Early market entry	Attract/retain key people
Holding companies 11 (5)	Niche marketing	Flexible service	Acquisitions	Investment/ new technology	Diversification
Retail 9 (4)	Niche marketing	Introduce new products	Diversification	Attract/retain key people	Flexible service
Total 100 (47)	Niche marketing	Attract/retain key people	Flexible service	Diversification	Early market entry

Phases in industry growth

As they develop industries pass through various phases which are classically described as embryonic, growth, maturity and decline. The characteristics of the three phases represented in the research sample, growth, maturity and decline, are shown in Tables 8.2 to 8.4. In this section we focus on the strategies which are used by supergrowth companies operating in industries at these separate stages of development.

The embryonic phase

We had expected that some of the sample would fall into the embryonic industry phase. But none of our sample companies fell into this category. The embryonic industries at this time were concerned with renewable energy sources, biotechnology or environmental management consultancy, as well as the more obvious high technology businesses in computing, robotics and automation, aerospace, telecommunications, new materials or the oil industry. The sample which we first identified included a couple of computer manufacturers. The first was Acorn, the company which produced the first BBC computer, which became widely used in the domestic and educational markets. The original sample also included Spectrum, which was a specialist distributor of personal computers. Both of these companies were in the personal computer market when it first emerged in Britain in the early 1980s. Over the period 1980 to 1985 these companies were star performers. The two companies achieved rates of sales growth and profit growth of around 96 per cent to 100 per cent per year compared with the sample average of about 40 per cent per year. However, during our initial field research in 1986 both of these companies failed due to the stresses and strains that such fast growth places on managers, staff and the business itself.

Strategies for 'growth phase' industries

It appears that industries in the 'growth' phase play host to medium-sized companies who are developers or 'packagers' of new products and services. They enter by capturing a specialized market niche and then maintain their lead by rapidly introducing new products and services to sell to the same segment. Amstrad was a prime example. The company grew by offering a hi-fi set for less than £100, which opened up a huge new market for 'affordable' hi-fi. This was followed by a series of follow-up products including personal computers, fax machines, satellite TV aerials and similar low-cost products for the home or small business markets.

At first these fast growing companies are managed by entrepreneurial leaders who function as the heads of all activities with trusted 'juniors' to support them. As the business grows the leaders of these companies either make the transition from being wholly entrepreneurial in their behaviour to becoming more 'professional' in their approach to management, or they are forced to recruit 'professional' managers. These 'professional' managers bring with them the experience of running divisions or medium-sized groups within larger companies and introduce structure and process to stabilize the growing business and enable delegation without losing control. Many of the most successful growth businesses operate with an entrepreneur and an 'administrator' working in partnership.

In companies which have to cope with new technologies and markets which are 'taking-off' there are many casualties and only a few winners. This is probably why our sample of successful mid-size companies contained few firms from embryonic industries. The general consensus on the failure of Acorn and Spectrum, for example, was that they had grown faster than their management teams could handle and that they were 'out-of-control'. They had failed to recognize that a rapidly growing business puts enormous stresses on its management team who have to increase their work rate and handle more transactions at all stages of the conversion process: sales,

Ta*ble* 8.2 Strategies for growth industries.

Company type	Growth strategy mix
Consumer electronics, telecommunications	Packaging of technology, flexible response, niche marketing, introducing new products, diversifying by customer group and region.
Sub-contracted services, consultancies	Early entry into new markets, acquisition, diversification, introduction of new services, niche marketing.
Package holidays	Tight financial controls, niche marketing, introducing new products, early entry into new markets.
Discount retailers	Regional expansion, tight controls, attract and retain key managers.
Manufacturers of racing engines, optical systems, electronic components	Acquisition, attract and hold high quality staff, invest in and apply new technology, tight financial controls, build on reputation of business.
Market research consultancies	Diversification into related products, acquisition, international expansion, enter early into growth markets, attract and hold quality staff.

purchasing, production, warehousing and delivery. In addition they also have to raise finance, recruit and train people, build or buy new facilities, and develop and test new products and introduce them to the market.

Strategies for the mature industry

It might be supposed that the mature and declining industries offered little scope for supergrowth. In fact there were a number of business which fell into each of these categories.

Firms in mature industries grew by acquiring other companies in the industry or by diversifying into 'growth' market niches. The lack of industry growth in general meant that they were not able to grow with a 'business as usual strategy' in a market which had peaked and now had a flat or very slow growth rate. In such situations growing the company meant:

1. Taking market share from weaker competitors.

2. Acquiring or merging with competitors.

3. Closing, turning around or divesting their less profitable and low-growth businesses.

4. Introducing new products targeted at specific market segments.

5. Investing in new technology to reduce costs and increase profitability and the price/quality attractiveness of their products.

In addition to their expansion in the UK they sought overseas partners or acquired overseas companies. Various aspects of export strategies are reviewed in Part 3.

Table 8.3 Strategies for mature industries.

Company type	Growth strategy mix
Paper manufacturer	Niche marketing, diversification into related products, acquisition, international expansion, attract and keep high-quality staff.
High quality printer	Attract and hold high-quality staff, be a low cost producer, flexible service to customers, international expansion, tight financial controls, acquisitions.

Strategies for declining industries

All the companies in this group had over 50 years' trading experience. They were generally family-owned with an outstanding reputation for a single product or set of products. However they were usually in the hands of a new management team drawn from outside the immediate family of the founder. In an attempt to improve their companies' growth prospects, the new managers were using 'niche marketing' strategies to help pull these companies out of the declining industries in which they found themselves.

Their initial strategy was to sell their existing products into new markets. To do so many of them had to automate their production methods to become more competitive in both price and quality. For example, a supplier of clothing to Marks and Spencer for over 30 years, had totally automated their design function using CAD/CAM technology. Another firm in the publishing business had diversified into up-market lists of books – including larger more expensive paperbacks. A third, a manufacturer of beds, had gone up-market into 'high-count pocket sprung beds' using imported technology.

Table 8.4 Strategies for declining industries.

Company type	Growth strategy mix
Publisher	International expansion, attract and hold quality staff, identify and serve niche markets, invest in and apply new technology, build on exclusive design or franchise.
Food manufacturer	Identify and serve a market niche, diversify into related markets or products, serve local markets, invest in and apply new technology, introduce a new product concept (create new market).
Industrial chemical holding company	Diversify into related products, access to technology through joint ventures, international expansion, identify and serve a market niche, build on exclusive design or franchise.
Retailer, wholesaler, printer	Build on exclusive design or franchise, diversify into related products, identify and serve a market niche, access to technology through joint ventures, introduce a new product concept.

Summary

The main strategies for growth could be summarized using the two categories applied in the first sections of this chapter:

1. Being selective in choosing both the market to enter and the strategic approach to be used.

2. Following this by adopting growth strategies which are a mixture of innovation, niche marketing, attracting and retaining good staff and managers, being flexible to and responding to customer needs and building partnerships and alliances with suppliers and customers.

In addition, some firms used a strategy of diversification into related areas of business where the same core competencies could be exploited in new markets. Tight financial control was also universally seen as an essential aid to successful growth.

The competitive strategies used in all instances by these supergrowth companies reflected the phase of growth of the industries in which they operated. The behaviour of managers running companies in 'growth' industries tended to be entrepreneurial and of high activity to cream every ounce of revenue and profit from the 'hunger' of the market. Those in 'mature' industries seem to be focused on reducing costs and gaining competitive advantage and profitability by being the lowest cost producers. Companies in 'declining' industries were seeking to optimize their investment in their existing business and diverting their gains to achieve a foot-hold in new markets. The management styles exhibited by the directors and owners of these companies also reflected the needs of the industries in which they operated.

The Merchant Retail Group case – growth issues in the home market

Introduction

The Merchant Retail Group, later the Normans Group, demonstrated many of the classic problems associated with attempts to grow rapidly in the home market. The company commenced operations as a commodity grower. By the mid-1980s it had developed a successful niche business in food and drink retailing. Although the total turnover was relatively small, the business was making a reasonable profit. The company was publicly owned with professional management.

1986: crisis and a new direction

The profits for 1986 were badly hit by two factors: the failure of the drinks business with its associated closing costs and increased pressure on margins in the commodity food products. The management then decided to embark on an expansion strategy based on developing the group's retail interests beyond its regional niche. As a result of implementing this strategy the group achieved profit and revenue growth in the region of 20 per cent per annum from 1986 to 1989.

1986-1989: a period of expansion

In 1986 the group acquired a regional chain of specialist food shops. Although the arrangement was described as a merger, it was financed by Merchant Retail through loans and a share issue. The acquired business continued to operate as an autonomous business. The management were retained and were asked to review all the specialist food operations of the combined group. On the basis of their recommendations the regional chain was expanded and several new branches were added.

Another specialist retailer was acquired in 1987. Again the acquisition was financed by share issue. This acquisition included a financial services company and considerable computer expertise.

During the same period some of the existing stores were being extended to take non-food merchandise. The emphasis within the core business was on margin improvement, routine refurbishment and where possible, the realization of economies of scale within the expanding group.

A further acquisition was made in 1988 when a chain of Scottish specialist food stores were purchased (to be managed by the team running the first acquisition). Also during that year a new non-executive director was appointed to advise on property matters – the property portfolio was now revalued to reveal a £10 million surplus.

In 1989 the group took a further step into diversification when it decided to invest £7 million in a new green-field retail site for non-food business including garden and DIY sections which were new sectors for the business. Additional management was employed to handle the development.

A small chain of furniture stores was also purchased that year. Most of the stores were sold off, with the remaining store being completely refurbished as a non-food store.

These developments were financed by a combination of long-term (£4 million) and short-term (£5 million) loans, guaranteed by the revalued property portfolio. This increased the group's gearing considerably, although some additional funds were obtained in the same year through the sale of the Scottish specialist food retailing chain that had continued to make losses.

1990: back into crisis

By 1990 the group was once again in trouble. The recession was starting to bite, sales were stagnant and profits were halved by interest payments on the loans. The chairman resigned in January 1990. The one bonus was the green-field site project – this was opened on time and was doing well. Despite the downturn in profits, a dividend was paid which was perhaps intended to reassure shareholders. The new chairman was appointed from within the existing management team. Figure 8.1 shows the company's results.

A strategy review carried out that year determined that the business should be cut back to its profitable core of original food stores and non-food specialist stores. All other activities were to be sold including the remaining specialist food business and activities like the in-house distribution service.

Difficult times continued through 1991 with sales down 7 per cent and continuing heavy interest payments. A rights issue of £6 million was made in order to reduce the gearing.

Conclusions

This case study echoes the story of many other businesses which set out to expand in the good times and then found themselves over-stretched when the recession arrived. The key lessons are:

- In the highly competitive retail markets a business can erect some competitive barriers by operating in a niche – either a

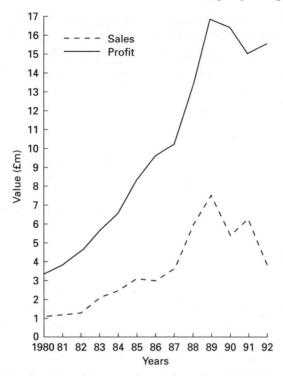

Figure 8.1 Merchant Retail Group – financial results 1980–1992.

geographical niche or in specialization. Although the intention was good – to grow by expanding into profitable niches – by coming out of its own niche the business was opened up to the full force of competition. A business which is neither in a niche nor one of the big operators is very vulnerable.

- Expansion requires a financial strategy aimed at retaining balance sheet strength. Expansion by borrowing can leave the company financially exposed with high interest payments to service.

- Success in developing a small regional retail business can be done with a small management team. The entrepreneurial skills used in creating organic growth are not necessarily those needed for managing acquisitions. Once expansion into other areas or other sectors occurs, considerable strain is put upon management. In particular, the differences experienced in operating in other geographical areas and in other, albeit related, sectors should never be under-estimated.

- The business of acquiring businesses requires its own special skills. In this case only one of three acquisitions delivered the profitability and growth potential expected and the others had to be resold at a considerable loss.

Growing a successful service business

Given the high proportion of supergrowth business in our research sample that fell either directly or indirectly into the service category, it was decided that some additional analysis would be carried out into successful growth strategies for this type of business.

The type of companies which fell into our category of service businesses within the sample were:

- Publishers of books and magazines
- Civil engineers
- House builders
- Companies managing hotels, public houses and casinos
- Package tour operators
- Security services businesses
- Firms offering sea transport
- Public relations companies
- Management consultancies

This sector grew apace in Britain during the 1980s and early 1990s. The high proportion of businesses in our sample reflected this even though banking, insurance and property were deliberately excluded. Sixty-three per cent of the companies involved in our research were in the direct services sector, including retail and distribution. A further 11 per cent were holding companies who typically engaged in both manufacturing and services. This left only 26 per cent of British supergrowth companies which were engaged mainly in manufacturing. The detailed breakdown is given in Figure 9.1.

Our research revealed nine strategic management systems or approaches which characterized the high growth services business. These were:

- Product policy
- Market segmentation
- Product/market diversification

Figure 9.1 Analysis of the supergrowth sample by industry sector.

- Flexibility
- Relationships with customers
- Production/operations policy
- Personnel and organization policy
- Management information and control systems
- Leadership style

In this chapter we explore how the high-growth companies in the services sector used these strategic management approaches to their advantage.

1 Product policy – early entry into growth markets

Early entry into growth markets proved an effective strategy for a number of medium-sized service businesses. We have termed this 'exploiting the window of opportunity'.

One company which offered services to businesses and public sector organizations attributed its 84 per cent compound growth over the initial five year period to taking advantage of the rapid changes which had occurred in office and industrial cleaning and in security services when public sector contracts were opened up to private companies.

Another organization which succeeded by grasping new opportunities quickly was a public relations consultancy. The management of this business attributed their success to 'The identification and exploitation of an industry vacuum and the provision of top quality service, creativity and commitment.' Again, in its initial five-year growth phase in the 1980s, the company grew at a rate of 217 per cent per annum, against an industry growth rate of some 20 per cent per annum in the same period.

2 Market segmentation – focusing on a market niche

Concentration on well-defined customer groups and offering them a package of products and services specially tailored to meet their needs emerged as a key to the success of many of the service companies which we visited. This would appear to be obvious, but it does require management to turn down business which does not fall within the defined area of focus. In a rapidly expanding business it requires a degree of discipline, and often courage, to turn away business.

This factor also means that management must take the time to analyse the business, to specify the areas of business focus and to communicate and enforce the resulting policy.

3 Product and market diversification

Exploiting new opportunities using the company's core skills was another strategy used by the organizations in our sample. The trick here seems to be modesty about management capabilities and trying to avoid 'the diversification too far'. This extra diversification, which is just outside the core competences of the management, then tends to become a millstone which absorbs a disproportionate amount of management time and resources and often ultimately jeopardizes the whole organization. The Stakis experience is a typical example of this type of 'over diversification'.

Another example of an apparently attractive diversification was shown by a company in the construction business which, because of the cuts in public expenditure for council housing, was prompted to use its core skills to enter the property development market which was buoyant during the early 1980s. The danger with this type of opportunistic diversification is that the company will have not faced a downturn in that new segment and may be caught out when the inevitable downturn arrives. Property development has been a market which has made millions for some, but has also left many substantial companies with severe problems when the market has turned down.

But the majority of our sample diversified successfully. The underlying mindset of these companies was their willingness to respond to market changes and moods rather than 'sticking to the knitting even when the knitted garment has no buyers'.

4 Flexibility

Most services businesses are not dependent on heavy capital investment. This means that they can respond quickly to market changes. The businesses in the sample were able to be more flexible because they operated like a federation of small businesses around product groups or project teams. Each product or project team could grow or contract as the need arose. They were also ready to move staff between units in response to changes in market demand.

The use of the 'star-shaped organization' (Figure 5.1), assisted this because it permits flexible development without providing space for the development of the kind of bureaucracy which stifles flexibility and the spirit of entrepreneurism.

5 Relationships with customers – creating long-term partnerships

Medium-sized companies are often dependent upon a few large corporations as customers. This dependency can be to the detriment of the medium-sized manufacturing businesses as the large business may be able to switch suppliers without harming their own stock position or their profitability. In the early 1980s, the climate of 'rampant Thatcherism' meant that many companies took a new and antagonistic approach to their suppliers. This hard attitude towards smaller suppliers during those tough economic times often resulted in the smaller business going out of business due to cash or profit starvation.

Service suppliers can be even more vulnerable because, during a recession, their contracts may be drastically reduced because they do not provide core products or essential components.

The security of the medium-sized business is therefore highly dependent on how well it manages its relationships with its customers. This means that the inter-relationship between the large and smaller company must be built on mutual dependency such that the services of the smaller firm are indispensable to the larger business. The more successful high-growth companies have turned the traditional supplier-customer relationship into a trading partnership with their customers so that they are seen as an integral part of their customer's business and company, e.g., their product development unit or their catering department.

This type of relationship does not only benefit the supplier. In many cases, for example, suppliers to major corporations have taken on the roles formerly taken by middle-management, or technical experts within the corporation, but now no longer present in the new 'slimmed-down' corporate structures. The type of customer relationships developed by Tallent Engineering as related in Chapter 1 exemplifies this style of customer relationship.

6 Production/operations policy – customer satisfaction depends upon employee commitment

Service companies depend on people rather than systems to meet their customer needs. In the words of one company director, contracting is, 'a people business. We are as good as our people are'. The chief executive of a publishing company said, 'we do have to make sure we have the right people on the editorial side'.

The emphasis and dependence on staff in service businesses is due to a realization that the quality of service and the satisfaction of customers are directly related. Managers in the successful service companies therefore sought to continuously build a committed workforce who focused on customer satisfaction and good customer relations. In this respect the staff in service businesses differ from their counterparts in manufacturing industry. The former experience daily contact with customers and the impact of their attitudes and behaviour have a direct effect on customer satisfaction. By contrast, in the manufacturing business, customer satisfaction is mainly reflected in acceptance of the product which acts as the 'real' interface between the customer and the organization. As a result the managers of successful service companies took time to build company pride in quality of service to ensure that the customers' needs were met whenever their staff and customers interacted.

7 Personnel and organization policy – attracting, keeping and motivating high-quality staff

Attracting and keeping high-quality staff seemed to be the greatest challenge to companies in the services sector. In many instances this was achieved through the use of:

- Profit-sharing schemes based on either individual or group performance.

- Open communication policies which enabled a free flow of information between the staff, their managers and the organization. Formal management briefings were complemented with more informal contact with staff often amounting to 'management by walk-about'. This technique not only provides a good downward communication medium, but also allows management to stay in touch with grass root events including changes in customer needs and demands.

- Management share-option schemes which made managers feel more committed to the company and which heightened their sense of 'ownership' of the business and its future.

- Internal promotion, where staff were nurtured, trained and offered promotion and by so doing made to feel that they had a career to aspire to within the organization. This is so much easier to do in a fast growing company although some companies resorted to 'buying-in' the skills rather than investing in their current employees.

- Staff training was used as a means of developing staff and of making them more effective in their work. Investment in training was seen as an investment in the future of a committed workforce.

- Where staff belonged to unions, managers saw that 'developing a win/win relationship with the unions was critical to (their) success'.

- Job enrichment and enjoyment was also seem as an important contributor to both motivation and performance of the staff. In the words of one manager, 'the company cannot succeed unless people are really enjoying what they are doing'. Enjoyment was defined more as job interest and challenge rather than 'fun at work'.

- Equity and fairness were an underlying theme in the successful high-growth companies, where the feeling of oneness was fostered. At Underwoods, the company's co-founder said, 'We built our business on giving customers and our staff a good deal. If you look after both, you achieve profits.'

8 Management information and control systems

In service businesses management information and control systems play a dual role. As in most businesses they support and help managers to keep their 'fingers on the pulse' through providing the necessary management information. But in addition, in service industries, information systems are used widely to support the staff by providing them with information to do their jobs. These 'front-end' systems allow staff to be empowered to deal with a wide range of customer situations without further reference. This strategy of putting responsibility for delivery of customer satisfaction in the hands of those most able to do so has therefore been enabled by the support of these systems. As a consequence we have seen these medium-sized businesses delivering the kind of service that is generally more associated with small owner-run businesses.

9 Leadership style

The leadership style of the service companies focused on building strong cultural values and an open and participative management style. An anecdote from one of the managers interviewed illustrates this well.

The managing director of a printing and publishing company 'walked the floor' every morning. One morning he was told by a printshop worker that the quality of the ink supplied to the company was poor. By afternoon the shop had a new source of supply of better quality ink.

This displays the presence of very open lines of communication and ease of access. Above all, we see demonstrated the high value placed by the MD on opinions from the shop floor. Knowing the staff who work for them is often a matter of pride with these leaders. It is a factor which wins employee recognition. The managing director of a firm of 200 employees said, 'I know virtually all of them and am visible to them. My own feeling is that with 200 people, I can know them all and what they are doing – there are no serried ranks doing production functions.'

The chairman of a travel company said: 'We are a big travel company that thinks like a small one. Everyone here is on a first name basis.' The same chairman encouraged participative decision-making and said: 'When I make an irrevocable decision, it is held for 24 hours in order that it can be improved by suggestions, then we know it is the 'right' solution for this business.' The attitude of this chairman shows that even big companies can keep the good habits of the successful medium-sized company.

Conclusion

Since the initial research phase was carried out we have seen a degree of convergence between the service and manufacturing sectors. Many of the most competitive manufacturing businesses have recognized the importance of delivering 'total customer service' rather than just being a product supplier. This does not only apply to those dealing with the retail trade where this type of approach is essential but also to businesses selling direct to the end user.

At the same time many service businesses have needed to 'productize' their services in order to replicate them for geographic expansion at home and abroad. This practice has been essential for businesses like the Body Shop where management have chosen to use franchising as a means of expansion. But it has by no means been confined to franchising businesses, and has been widely seen as a way of maintaining the business culture and values for use in new markets.

Introduction

The original study was sponsored by the Anglo-German Foundation in order that comparisons could be made between UK and West German experiences in the early 1980s. During that period, although both countries faced the common problem of declining basic industries, like ship-building, steel and textiles, with its concomitant unemployment, West Germany's industrial and economic growth outpaced Britain's. This was achieved in spite of the relatively high value of the Deutschmark against other currencies.

As in Japan, West German industry had been developing steadily for more than 20 years, continuing the momentum produced by the post-war re-building programme. During that time, in contrast to the UK's see-sawing political and economic environment, West Germany had experienced political stability, no balance of payments crisis – or run on the Deutschmark – and steady economic growth. Again, like the Japanese, the German 'miracle' was based on export-led industry with a reputation for technical excellence and high quality.

We were therefore interested to see whether this more stable economic environment would affect the profile of high-growth mid-size businesses.

The study

The German study was carried by Professor Dr Dietger Hahn, his research assistant, Herr Ulrich Gräb, and other colleagues at the Justus Liebig University in Giessen. Their work, which was carried out in conjunction with the Henley team, was published in 1987 by the Institut für Unternehmungsplanung (IUP), Geissen under the title, *Wachstumsstrategien Erfolgreicher Mittelständischer Unternehmungen*[1].

From the start differences became apparent. In the UK, databases containing five-year financial histories were readily accessible and it was relatively easy to locate companies that satisfied the supergrowth criteria. It was then possible to structure a sample of 47 companies by industry sector and by geographical spread. In Germany, there are fewer publicly owned mid-size companies – the German stock market caters mainly for large businesses – and financial information is far harder to come by. The German sample was finally selected through the help of local chambers of commerce and numbered 22 companies.

The information-gathering approaches used were as follows:

1. Databases covering both private and publicly owned mid-sized companies are readily available in the UK but not in Germany where most mid-size concerns are private firms funded by banks.

2. The UK sample was a structured sample, whereas the German sample was unstructured – selected from company names provided by the chambers of commerce.

3. The interviewers in the UK and in Germany used the same structured questionnaire.

4. Company financial records were made available to the researchers in the UK, but detailed records were not generally made available in Germany.

The difficulty in obtaining detailed information about businesses in Germany (which also applies to other continental European countries), compared with the ready access to data about British and American companies, is a significant problem faced by those British companies with ambitions to expand into mainland Europe.

Comparison of the samples

From an initial comparison of statistics some basic differences between the two samples became apparent. These related to ownership, size of the business (judged by turnover) and industry type.

Ownership and financing

Table 10.1 shows the ownership profile of the two samples.

Table 10.1 Ownership of supergrowth businesses in the UK and Germany.

Type	UK (%)	Germany (%)
Private	34	91
Public	66	9
Total:	100	100

The fact that two-thirds of the UK sample were publicly owned compared with less than 10 per cent in Germany highlights the contrasting patterns of business ownership and financing. In Germany banks play a major role in providing long-term business finance for medium-sized companies and they become far more involved in the business than their UK counterparts. For example, they will often have a board representative. This is partly due to the presence of regional banks (these really have no direct equivalents in the UK) which have strong links with the community and are keen to support local wealth creation. Thus the normal medium-sized business is family-owned and financed by local banks.

In the UK, the banks supply working capital, venture capital companies and investment banks supply development capital, and long-term capital is provided by the capital markets including the London Stock Exchange and the Unlisted Securities Market. The capital markets are generally open to medium-sized businesses (for the purposes of this study, defined as those companies with an annual sales turnover of between £10m and £100m in 1984/85) in the UK, but public ownership accompanies the provision of such funds. One incentive for such companies to seek public money has been the relatively high and fluctuating cost of bank borrowing in the UK which can be difficult to plan for and manage. With public ownership also comes the requirement to provide shareholder information through prospectuses and annual and interim reports.

Large and medium-sized businesses in Britain tend to lose their links with local sources of capital. For example, when Rowntree, with its strong identification with York, was sold to Nestlé, the employees were concerned about the potential adverse effect on the community. But the institutional shareholders had no particular loyalty to the region. The problem

135

with public funding is the requirement of shareholders (in particular institutional shareholders) for short-term profits. A number of companies like the Really Useful Group and Virgin have been taken out of public ownership by their founders who wished to avoid taking actions that they felt were not in the best long-term interests of the business.

Size

The companies in the German sample were, in general, smaller than those in the UK sample as measured by annual turnover (see Table 10.2). Sixty-four per cent had sales of less than £25 million in 1984/85, whereas in the UK sample 64 per cent of the firms had sales revenues between £25m and £100m.

Table 10.2 Annual turnover in 1984/5 for supergrowth companies in the UK and Germany.

Turnover (£m)	UK		Germany	
	Number	Per cent	Number	Per cent
Up to £25m	17	36	14	64
£25 to £50m	16	34	6	27
£50 to £100	14	30	2	9
Total	47	100	22	100

Type of industry sector

Although the service sector had been growing in Germany, the majority of the companies in the German sample were in manufacturing. However, in the UK sample, manufacturing firms were only 25 per cent of the total. This sector weighting partially accounts for the differences in strategic approach between the two countries.

Key findings

The role of technology

For many years technology has been accepted in Germany as the basis for 'the German miracle'. The German businessmen tend to believe (like the Swedes and the Danes) that an affluent society is built upon value added through the application of new technology. German industry is therefore committed to investment in technology and companies like Siemens, Bosch,

BMW, Daimler-Benz, and Volkswagen have become world market leaders based on use of technology.

At the same time a large number of successful medium-sized businesses have developed which work as partners to these large international businesses and a number of these were identified in the German sample. These businesses supply components, machinery and expertise as part of a long-term relationship with their customers. They thought the following attributes were necessary to maintain such a relationship:

- access to the latest technology
- a high degree of efficiency
- good quality standards, and
- close contact with the customer

This relationship requires close collaboration, particularly for new technical developments. This co-operative attitude contrasts strongly with the 'adversarial' and 'arm's length' supplier/buyer relationship advocated as part of the British notion of a market economy. Some of the British companies also worked closely with their customers, e.g. suppliers to Marks and Spencer or B&Q. But in the British sample there were no component suppliers to the automotive industry. Also we found no evidence of high-growth medium-sized businesses co-operating with British universities or polytechnics.

In Germany there are also close links between the companies and the technical universities, in areas such as computer-aided design and computer-integrated manufacturing.

Ownership and the community

The difference in ownership and financing has a significant effect on development strategies. In Germany the commercial banks take a strategic stake in businesses and consider that they have an equal commitment to the companies which they invest in, as well as to the customers who provide the funds. The regional nature of many of these banks is just one of the ways in which business appears much closer to the local community in Germany. One chief executive stated that the most important thing they had done was to build a sports stadium for the town. The firms are therefore embedded in the community in a way that UK firms are not.

The role of innovation

In Britain two-thirds of the supergrowth enterprises were in the service sector as the manufacturing sector declined through not being able to compete with international rivals. This inability to compete was brought about by a combination of factors including poor industrial relations, insufficient investment in new technology and a lack of customer focus. Sinclair and Acorn, two high-technology companies which were selected for the original sample, failed and were taken over by their competitors.

Many British high-technology business start-ups occurred. University 'science parks' encouraged the setting up of new ventures in technology. The question is 'Why did these high technology start-ups not become new mid-size high-growth companies?' It appears that many of the inventors and designers simply did not want to take on the burdens of manufacturing[2]. They preferred to offer the fruits of their work as a service or under licence. Many high-technology businesses found that they could not sell their inventions in the UK and therefore sold to German, Japanese or American firms. Boots Celltech, for example, a pioneer of biotechnology was initially funded by the MRC (Medical Research Council) but found difficulty in licensing its new technology to British companies.

To our surprise there were no high-technology companies in the UK sample whereas the success of many of the 22 German supergrowth businesses was based on new process or product technology. They see innovation as the basis for success.

In the British firms flexibility was considered more important than innovation. This probably reflects the need for British firms to cope with a more volatile business environment.

Sources of growth

One source of high growth potential in the German firms was their symbiotic relationship with major manufacturers over a long period. This usually generates sustainable growth built upon manufacturing expertise. By contrast much of the growth in the UK companies, in particular for those in service businesses, was opportunistic. The main, and possibly short-lived, opportunities that occurred in the early 1980s were:

- In sectors experiencing a *boom*, e.g. construction, leisure and tourism.

- In sectors undergoing *consolidation*, e.g. at the time the publishing and food wholesaling businesses were subject to acquisition and consolidation. At such times businesses grow at the expense of others, rather than by generating new growth.

- In sectors undergoing *transformation*, e.g. the contracting out of services by both local and central government created opportunities for the creation of new services to business in areas like cleaning, catering, computer maintenance, management consultancy, public relations and market research.

- *Rejuvenated companies* operating in mature markets. Typically rejuvenation occurred when professional management was introduced into family firms such as Liberty's.

For new British companies there can be a problem entering the markets. Many of our markets are dominated by a few large companies with massive buying power. The supermarkets, for example, exercise considerable control in the UK over the market for food products. It is extremely difficult for a new entrant to break into the grocery market, build a reputation and then diversify. Some firms like Marks and Spencer do work in collaboration with their suppliers over a period although they do not offer long-term contracts.

The argument for such 'vertical partnerships' between small suppliers and large customers is clear. Smaller businesses are good at innovation, product development and market penetration. Large companies can provide access to distribution systems, cheap finance, economies of scale, management and technical expertise, etc. But this type of close collaboration does not fit in with the adversarial approach of the 'market economy'. 'Partnership' implies the use of preferred suppliers rather than open tenders based purely on price. In Germany, large companies will make loans to long-term suppliers who need to invest in R&D or re-equip in order to improve quality or cost-effectiveness.

Japanese and German manufacturers treat their main suppliers as part of an 'extended family' with many common objectives. In the 1990s British component suppliers are entering into partnerships with Nissan, Toyota and Honda; and Ford, Vauxhall and Rover are working closely with 'preferred suppliers'. But real partnership is based on trust and takes some time to develop.

Dealing with risk

The British business environment is quite volatile:

- The economy fluctuates.
- The banks foreclose when cash flow gets tight.
- Shareholders disinvest if short-term results are poor.
- The government stands off – to allow the market economy to work – and lets the weakest companies go to the wall.
- Large businesses deal with suppliers on an adversarial basis and many regard suppliers as a good source of credit.

This makes British firms vulnerable and subject to failure. It is hardly surprising that new businesses in that environment are mostly based in service industries where capital investment needs are lower than for high-technology firms and more flexibility is possible.

British companies also are seldom closely linked to a local community like the German businesses. Those local businesses that remain are gradually being swallowed up by national enterprises. For example, regional brewers are being taking over by national chains, and the same process is happening with local department stores and hotels.

In Germany, which has experienced a much more stable post-war economy, company roots run deep. For example, most regions have a local brewer; Lich Brewery serves the area around Lich in Hesse and has a 90 per cent market share. They have a loyal customer base, a loyal work force, and the owners live in the area.

Barriers to growth

The barriers to growth vary by type of business. To grow in the manufacturing sector, a firm needs to have specialized product or process knowledge and to make a capital investment in plant and equipment in order to be competitive in cost and quality. In service businesses, the barriers to entry are more concerned with gaining market share through developing a reputation and beating the competition on customer service. Table 10.3 shows how chief executives saw the barriers to growth in Britain and Germany.

Ta*ble* 10.3 Barriers to growth: ranking by chief executives in Britain and Germany.

Ranking	UK	Germany
1	Competition, monopolies	Regulations, import restrictions, protectionism
2	Establishing goodwill and reputation	Performance at acceptable standards
3	Lack of managerial talent	Warranties and product or service liabilities
4	Capital investment, funding	Patents and licences
5	Licences, planning permission	Specialized product/service know-how
6	A combination of the factors above	Capital intensive plants and processes to deliver economies of scale

Note: Most of the British firms were service businesses and most of the German firms were in manufacturing.

Strategic profiles

Table 10.4 provides a summary of responses to questions on the strategies adopted by British and German companies. The only difference is the timing of market entry, where the Germans considered it important to be first to market, whereas this was not considered vital by the UK firms. Once again this highlights a difference between manufacturing and service sectors. In product-based businesses much rides on being first to market with new products. This establishes both market leadership and, often, legal protection through patents. In service businesses it is not necessarily important to be first, but it is important to offer a competitive service.

Otherwise the strategy profiles for supergrowth businesses are similar:

1. Enter the market early.

2. Focus on a market niche (defined in terms of a customer group and a product type).

141

3. Introduce new products and new processes.

4. Stay independent.

5. Establish leadership in quality (but control costs).

6. Charge a premium price.

Table 10.4 Comparison of UK and German strategy profiles.

Strategic factor	Alternative strategies			
1. Timing of entry	First to market	G	B	Second to market
2. Marketing strategy	Market niche	G/B		Total market
3. Product strategy	Innovation	G/B		Imitation
4. Process strategy	Innovation	G/B		Imitation
5. Focus on co-operation	Joint venture Acquisition		G/B	Autonomy
6. Quality relative to others	Leader	G/B		Follower
7. Cost	Low		G/B	Not low
8. Price	High	G/B		Low

G = German result and B = British result.

Conclusion

Although the business leaders in the two countries recognize similar success characteristics and common barriers to growth, the overall development pattern is quite different. High-growth mid-sized companies in Germany largely occur in the manufacturing sector where by acting in collaboration with larger partners they lead the technological advancement of products and processes. In Britain, high-growth companies are predominantly service-based, where they are less dependent upon major investment and can maintain the flexibility to deal with the historically fluctuating UK economy.

Whilst deregulation and freer competition in the UK appear to have made British companies more competitive, the emphasis on self-reliance and confrontational negotiation appears ill-suited to the development of high-technology manufacturing industries. The major German manufacturers, like their counterparts in Japan, do not make progress alone, but as leaders of a 'partnership' including suppliers, employees, local and central government and university business schools. If Britain is going to retain any significant manufacturing capability there are lessons to be learned from the German experience.

In Germany growing businesses have access to long-term capital from regional banks; they benefit from long-term partnerships with world-class manufacturing companies; they have access to leading-edge technology through technological universities and research institutes; they have government support in research and development and export promotion.

Britain's growing enterprises need similar types of help but it is not forthcoming. British industry's relationship with government seems to oscillate between a complete 'arm's length' relationship and close direction, without reaching a happy medium. The British banks advertise their help but often have a ruthless approach to smaller businesses. Financial institutions put the interest of their shareholders first. Large companies, in general, seem to regard their suppliers as adversaries rather than partners. Technological and market support for British industry in no way compares with the help available for growing businesses in Germany, Japan or the USA.

Notes

1 Dietger Hahn and Ulrich Gräb (1987) *Wachstumsstrategien Erfolgreicher Mittelständischer Unternehmungen*, Institut für Unternehmungsplanung (IUP), Geissen.
2 Segal, Quince, Wicksteed & Fraunhofer Institute (1987) *New Technology Based Firms ... in West Germany and the United Kingdom*, Anglo-German Foundation, London.

Part 3
Can mid-size companies thrive internationally?

Part 3 provides details of the research undertaken at Henley Management College to examine the international strategies of supergrowth companies, the results of which are summarized in Chapter 11. The studies, which were sponsored by Price Waterhouse, complement the earlier studies of high-growth medium-sized companies reported in Part 2.

The contents of the chapters in this section are as follows:

Chapter 11
Going international: the evidence for international success - Brent Chemicals International
The summary of the research results in this area, including the reasons why companies sometimes need to exercise this growth option.

Chapter 12
Case studies of international experiences
Summarizes the strategies and leadership styles used by a number of representative companies drawn from the database.

Chapter 13
Building an international bridgehead
Explains the entry strategies used by these companies in order to move into international markets.

Chapter 14
Taking a service business overseas
Explores the special problems faced by service businesses in developing internationally.

Going international – how mid-size companies succeed 11

In the original study we found that a number of supergrowth companies chose overseas development as a key element of their growth strategy. This prompted a new set of questions to research as outlined below.

Why go for overseas expansion?

The barriers

The experiences of large British businesses, many of which have struggled to succeed in overseas markets, have shown some of the main export sales difficulties:

- Britain's island position has historically presented a natural physical barrier to expansion for domestic companies with high-growth ambitions.

- The average British manager's lack of understanding of foreign languages and cultures compared with many of their continental counterparts seems to present a particular difficulty.

- Despite the EC and GATT treaties, import tariffs and a host of similar protectionist measures remain common in both Europe and further afield. A report by Coopers and Lybrand for the Department of Industry in 1989[1] indicated that British companies faced major barriers to expanding through acquisition in mainland Europe (in the period 1984–1989 British investment in Europe amounted to £7.5 billion compared with European investment in Britain of £12.3 billion).

Given that medium-sized businesses by definition have limited resources – in particular they have limited finances to fund development and usually have a small management team with little experience in dealing with foreign conditions – it has to be realized that international business requires special initiative and drive.

147

The benefits

Despite these barriers there are powerful reasons why some medium-sized companies need to contemplate such a move:

- When high-growth medium-sized companies reach the natural ceiling of market potential within their chosen niche in the UK they are faced with the choice of either developing new expertise in their domestic market or exploiting the same business niche overseas. Dealing with products, services, or technologies that you know in new but similar markets can often be an easier option than developing new ideas for the domestic market.

- The European Community with its population of some 300 million and what Kenichi Ohmae describes as the 'triad' – the global market of the USA, Japan and Europe with some 700 million consumers – represents a significant increase on the UK's 55 million.

- With the increasing threat of foreign competition in most markets, one strategy for meeting competition is 'to get your retaliation in first'. This means taking on overseas competitors in their own markets – putting them on the defensive – rather than waiting for them to attack you in your home market.

- Good communication, cheap transportation, and the widespread use of English as a business language are all factors which assist UK businesses which choose to export.

- Increased globalization means that international businesses are increasingly looking for service providers capable of supporting them world wide. Brent Chemicals, which features as a case study at the end of this chapter, has built its business using a strategy based on this factor.

- Some companies gain access to new technology, ideas and approaches through contact with overseas markets. For example, exporting to Germany should provide access to their technical engineering developments. Similarly computer businesses might well want to keep in touch with the west coast of America.

Our approach

We were particularly keen to study medium-sized high-growth companies with a successful international business so that we could examine how they had achieved this overseas success. A special study was carried out to investigate the management approaches and business strategies which were adopted by high-growth medium-sized companies operating in international markets. A new database consisting of 334 qualifying medium-sized high-growth companies was created from the computer databases used in our main study. The qualifying criteria were updated to reflect the later time span used. This time medium-sized firms were defined as having a turnover of between £20 million and £200 million. In the five-year period studied these companies averaged 39 per cent per annum sales growth and 57 per cent per annum growth in profits.

The key questions – what we wanted to know

- What kind of business were they and where did they operate?
- Which markets did they enter?
- What entry strategy did they employ? For example, did they export directly, licence, establish a branch or subsidiary, use an agent, acquire a company or form a joint venture?
- How did they compete?
- What leadership style did they adopt?
- How did they internationalize the basic functions of the company: manufacturing, purchasing, product development, marketing, etc.?
- How did they manage and control the overseas business?
- What organizational changes did they make?
- What were the implications for the directors of the business?

Summary of results

What kind of businesses were they and where did they operate?

One hundred and forty-seven (44 per cent) of the 334 firms in the database reported substantial overseas sales. Table 11.1 shows the higher proportion of product, and combined product and service businesses, than pure service businesses in the exporting firms than in the non-exporters.

Figure 11.1 shows how the proportion of exporting businesses varied by trade sector.

Ta*ble* 11.1 Comparison of exporting and non-exporting businesses by type. The table shows that it is more difficult for service-based businesses to export than product-based ones

	Manufacturing companies	*Manufacturing and service companies*	*Service companies*
Non-exporters (187)	11%	9%	80%
Exporters (147)	29%	26%	45%

In addition to the service sector businesses in general, a number of specific trade sectors find exporting difficult. For example:

- *Building contractors* face difficulties because overseas construction methods differ markedly.

- *Distribution* – e.g. motor distributors – where local franchise agreements with major manufacturers limit expansion boundaries.

- *Retailing and wholesale distribution*, which has proved difficult even for the largest multiples such as Marks and Spencer and Sainsbury.

Other services such as leisure businesses including public houses, hotels and fast food outlets are tailor-made for the domestic market and therefore face a difficult culture barrier in moving overseas. Business services such as management consultancy and advertising agencies seem to fare rather better.

The geographic bias of exporting businesses

The greatest proportion of exporting firms were London or home counties based (50 per cent), although this area accounts for only 17 per cent of the population. The north-east was also over represented with a combined 30 per cent of the database (but only 16 per cent of the population). Despite the work of the development agencies in Wales, Scotland and Northern Ireland their proportion at 4 per cent (with 10 per cent of the population) was disappointingly low.

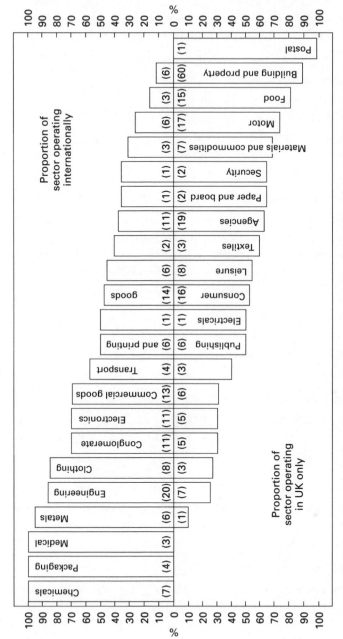

Figure 11.1 Distribution between exporters and non-exporters by trade sector. Source: Herbect and Taylor, 1990.

151

The ownership profile

There was a distinct difference in the profile of ownership between UK-only operators which were 40 per cent privately owned and the overseas traders only 14 per cent of which were in private hands.

The level of overseas sales

Of the 147 exporters only 90 published export figures. Of the 90, 56 (63 per cent) had overseas sales accounting for more than 20 per cent of their total sales and 17 (20 per cent) had overseas sales amounting to more than 50 per cent of their sales revenue being exported.

Target export markets

Traditionally British businesses have traded strongly with Commonwealth countries where English is spoken, and an English legal system applies. However, in the 90 firms reporting on export sales, Europe was the top target (48 per cent) and the USA the second target (35 per cent).

The results from personal interviews

In addition to the analytical information reported above, the following key observations were gained from interviewing the business leaders.

Leadership style

All the leaders interviewed had had an international business career in larger companies prior to attaining their current position. All believed that their industries were international in scope and that, as a consequence, their businesses needed to be international as well. As leaders they operated internationally on a personal basis, travelling extensively (often spending about a third of their time abroad) and usually they spoke foreign languages.

Organization development

The leaders recognized three stages of organization internationalization. These are shown in Table 11.2.

Stage III required international business units staffed by international employees.

Table 11.2 Three stages of organization internationalization.

Stage I	Stage II	Stage III
Direct export from the UK base	Set up overseas subsidiaries	Create an international HQ
Exploit niches in other markets	Duplicate niche businesses	Develop global niches

Method of export expansion

All the companies interviewed expanded through overseas acquisition, a major reason for which was their need to buy local management. The leaders recognized that they had made substantial time investments in developing their overseas businesses. They also recognized that this could affect both the domestic business and the leaders' personal lives. The leader cannot continue to manage the day-to-day business of the domestic company and lead the drive for overseas development.

The barriers to overcome in developing service businesses overseas

The following barriers were recognized as major obstacles to overcome:

• The need to safeguard technology and know-how.

• Establishment of a guaranteed standard quality of service for the company or the brand.

• Creation of a competitive advantage in a foreign market.

• Re-creation of the personal interaction which service businesses depend upon. This involves:
  – local knowledge
  – networks of contacts
  – an understanding of local customer needs
  – leveraging size to gain buying discounts, recruit good staff and receive quality service from suppliers.

Overcoming the barriers to successful exporting

The managers of these successful exporting supergrowth businesses identified a number of approaches that have proven successful in overcoming barriers to exporting:

1. *The packaging of key elements as products* For example training may be offered in self-contained packages with 'train the trainer' courses to support it. Similarly computer software has largely been 'productized'. In each case the service is better protected and the need for staff support is reduced.

2. *Licences and franchises used to package the whole business* A full package for the licensee will include full service support from the provision of supplies through marketing and design to management information systems. Examples of successful businesses operating in this way include the Body Shop, Benetton, McDonald's and Holiday Inn.

3. *Creating a competitive advantage through technology* Examples of this are provided by marketers of databases, many of which have been exploited successfully in areas such as:
   - customer behaviour (e.g. Nielsen)
   - company strategies (e.g. PIMS)
   - communications (e.g. travel, banking)
   - marketing (mailing lists)

4. *Personal interaction* Individuals who are key to a business create their own competitive advantage if they can achieve 'star' status, e.g. Peter Drucker, Tom Peters and Michael Porter in management development

5. *Internationalizing the strategic vision* The company philosophy, the organization and the people must all have an international perspective. The leader must make the vision international so that it can be understood in all cultures but still retain its vigour and create the right environment in each subsidiary.

6. *Maintaining product or service flexibility* This enables tailor-making by local agents or management in order to match local market needs. For example, facsimile transmission now facilitates the production of local editions of the *Financial Times* in Europe.

7. *International alliances and partnerships* These operate with local companies in order to:
   - reduce entry investment costs,
   - overcome cultural and language barriers, and
   - obtain access to established distribution channels.

8. *Building direct consumer loyalty* This is especially important when dealing through agents, for example by creating an international club – as the airlines do. It is vital when using agents to develop product champions within the agent's organization.

It is clear that it is generally far more difficult to export services because of the heavy dependency on the personal aspect. The UK's move to a service-based economy has raised this issue as a major problem for the late 1990s.

Brent Chemicals International – an international growth strategy

Introduction

The early growth of the Brent Manufacturing Company Limited was linked closely to that of Rolls Royce's aero division. Brent worked closely with Rolls Royce to develop a non-destructive testing system for jet engines. The resulting Ardrox products became standard maintenance products for engine cleaning and testing. As aircraft with Rolls Royce engines were sold around the world, so Brent set up a series of licencees, distributors and joint venture companies to service the maintenance requirements. Over time the company had expanded into a variety of speciality chemical markets including: food and beverage plant sanitization, industrial metal finishing, chemicals for printed circuit board and semi-conductor manufacturing processes, inks and coatings and other pre-press services primarily for the packaging industry and automotive body pre-treatment. A window of opportunity arose for Brent and other similar medium-sized businesses to acquire small speciality chemical businesses as many larger chemical companies shed non-core activities in order to concentrate on economic production of large-bulk products.

Creating an international strategy

When Bill Cross first joined the company in 1970 his task was to rationalize this network of businesses which had 'growed like Topsy' and create a long-term strategy for international growth. Since that time the management have worked with various business school professors both to raise the management's planning and strategic thinking abilities and to create a clear corporate direction.

On examining the business it was apparent that the company was operating in global niche markets and that, in order to survive, the company had to be global too. The strategy was therefore to serve customers either on a global basis (aerospace and electronics) or on a pan-European basis. This simple statement became the fundamental driver for strategy development and it had many implications: from simple issues like changing the name – to Brent Chemicals International – to more complex issues like the future of the product portfolio.

Some of the key steps taken included:

- An early step was to start to regain control of international operations. Many of the European operations were then created by extracting Ardrox activities, together with key personnel, from the various partnerships.

- The multinational management teams developed for the aerospace industry were then used as a focus for extending industrial metal finishing and electronics activities. The inks, coatings and pre-press service activities were developed separately and in parallel, but also using the international business. The company has used a mixture of organic growth and acquisition to develop the chosen niches. These international management teams operated in a decentralized way.

- It became apparent that two businesses, the food and beverage plant sanitization and automotive body pre-treatment, were limited to their respective UK markets with little prospect for successful expansion overseas. These were therefore disposed of although they represented some 25 per cent of turnover at the time.

- This action left the business with five core business areas, each with above average international growth prospects.

As the drive for 'internationalization' has continued in the company, attention has become more and more focused on developing international management to match the business profile of the company. The 1990 sales analysis shows that only 36 per cent of sales now stem from the UK, 41 per cent come from continental Europe, 20 per cent from North America and 3 per cent from Asia. In 1991 the two senior operating directors supporting Bill Cross's successor Stephen Cuthbert could both speak four continental European languages and all senior management can speak, or are learning, another language. The intention is to create a truly international management team and to bolster the board by appointing 'non-Brits'.

Within Europe the company changed in 1990 from a country-based structure to one based on business units, so that European customers could be served on a pan-European basis which in many cases reflected the way in which the customers themselves were moving. This step should lead to the creation of world-wide business groups, starting with aerospace and electronics. The North American and Far East groups have been structured with this in mind.

Conclusions

Brent Chemicals International with their strategic focus on pursuing international service niches created a successful medium-sized business (turnover around £100 million in 1990) in an industry otherwise dominated by large companies. They are respected by their customers (and competitors) for the quality of their products, people and service. Their plan is to grow sales to some £500 million by the year 2000 and they have a clear strategy to achieve this. They believe that their structure, their culture and their clear focus allow them to be 'one step ahead of the customers and two steps ahead of competition' – and they mean to keep it that way.

In summary, the company shows that being international is more a 'state of mind' rather than a matter of size or resources – and that success in international markets does need a continuing commitment to create the level of business that enables full and equal attention to be given to the needs of international customers.

Notes

Coopers and Lybrand (1989) *Barriers to Takeover in the EC*, HMSO.

Case studies of international experiences

12

This chapter relates the experiences reported by managers from six supergrowth companies which have succeeded in developing substantial overseas businesses in the late 1980s and early 1990s (see Table 12.1). The original research was carried out by Lesley Hughes through an interview programme aimed at gaining responses to a set of key questions listed in Table 12.2.

Table 12.1 The case study companies.

	Business type	Key interviewee	Fifth year turnover (£m)	Turnover: average growth (5 years) (%)	Profit: average growth rate (5 years) (%)
Successful					
1	Clothing design and distribution	MD	72	68	74
2	Packaging and chemical manufacture	Chief executive	149	22	33
3	Public relations agency	Director	68	75	89
4	Manufacturing mini-conglomerate	Chairman	178	111	99
5	Computer services bureau	Chairman and chief executive	39	21	35
Unsuccessful					
6	Sales promotion agency	MD	21	51	66

The companies and their leaders

Internationally experienced 'professional entrepreneurs'

The leaders of these businesses were male, entrepreneurial professionals – the 'professional entrepreneurs' identified in the earlier studies. In many cases they had trained with 'blue-chip' companies, for example the chief executive of the packaging

Table 12.2 International markets: how do medium-sized companies succeed?

Leadership style	Are there particular leadership styles which are common to businesses with significant international operations?
Company strategy	How do successful companies operate in international markets? How is international business featured in the companies' overall business plan for growth?
Market choice	How and on what criteria do companies choose the international markets which they enter?
Entry strategy	What strategies are employed for entering new overseas markets? What barriers are encountered when expanding internationally and how are they overcome?
Organizational structure and process	How do these companies organize themselves for overseas growth?
Implementation and control	How do successful international firms implement and control their chosen strategies?
The single European market	How do these companies perceive the effects of the single European market? What steps have they taken to protect themselves from threats and to exploit such opportunities as may arise?

and chemicals business had been the director of an international division of GKN. Furthermore, their experience and training was not confined to the UK. In all cases, the leaders of the companies had practical experience of overseas trade. For example, the director of the public relations agency had previously conducted business in both the USA and the Pacific basin.

In general, these senior executives spent a large amount of time travelling. Before acquiring a Japanese subsidiary, the director of the PR firm went to Japan 18 times in 15 months 'to meet and get to know the people and to ensure harmonious relations'. These men do not complain about the amount of business travel they undertake; they seem to enjoy business travel and regard it as a normal part of their lives, although it can have a significant impact on their domestic and family life. The over-riding impression that they created was that they had a vision of their companies as being 'international businesses'. The leader of the sales promotion company where one overseas venture had 'failed' was also a 'committed internationalist', however there were some important differences in approach in this venture which will be examined later.

Company strategies

Niche markets

All the companies interviewed were national rather than regional operators in their home market. Each of them also competed in a defined niche market.

The focus of the public relations business, for example, was on 'PR proper' and not on the broad range of marketing services offered by many of their competitors. The chairman's mission was to 'establish a world-wide PR network providing the highest quality standards'.

In all cases, with the exception of the unsuccessful venture, the companies competed in the same market niche overseas as they did at home.

The unsuccessful sales promotion company acquired an overseas business that was operating in a completely different market niche to the rest of the group. The managing director said, 'we failed to stick to our strategy which was to develop, by acquisition, in closely related business areas'. The acquisition which had problems was a marketing consultancy, which operated in an area of marketing where they were inexperienced.

By sticking to their core products or services the other firms were able to expand internationally while keeping their risks to a minimum.

Competing on value, not price

In common with other studies, 'competing on value not price' was common practice with all six firms. The managing director of the clothing company related how his company had revolutionized the UK jeans market by introducing a new fabric which was of a much higher quality than his competition and quality became his company's watchword.

Internationalizing the whole business

The research showed that the firms took an international approach to more than just sales and marketing and were prepared to go international in other areas like purchasing, production and recruitment. The packaging manufacturer sourced the steel for its drums from a selection of six suppliers across Europe, and had production plants throughout the Continent.

All the companies recruited foreign nationals to work in their overseas companies. None said that they would consider selecting a British expatriate to run a foreign company.

Adapting to local markets

There is much debate in the literature about the relative merits of 'localization' versus 'globalization' of products and services for international business. This study showed that, without exception, where services were involved, the services provided were invariably tailored to local market conditions. Correspondingly, an accurate interpretation of local customer requirements is an important pre-requisite to successful service provision.

Overseas market entry

We had assumed that the stimulus for overseas expansion would have arisen from market saturation or slower growth in the home market. This did not prove to be the case. The main reasons given were either:

1. The ambition of the chief executive or chairman to achieve international growth, or
2. a chance development, e.g. when the business acquired another UK business with existing overseas interests.

A *vision for international growth*

Three of the companies initially became involved in international business through the ambition of a leader. The clothing company, for example, was a family-run business led by an entrepreneur, who initially recommended the USA as a new distribution market because it was a 'challenge' rather than on the basis of detailed market research or sophisticated analysis. When a non-family chairman was appointed at a later stage, further international expansion occurred on a more methodical basis.

In the case of the public relations business the choice of the market to enter – the USA – was made because it was an essential step in being recognised as a world-wide operator, what might be called the 'Madison Avenue' effect.

International growth, by 'accident'

The three remaining firms became international operators through acquisition. In each case the international operations of the acquired company were not the principal reasons for making the deal.

The computer services company purchased a competitor for its UK network, but the business also included a number of northern European outlets and these were seen as a 'bonus'. Similarly, the packaging and chemicals company found itself exporting to Europe when it bought back its own shares and other business interests from a major shareholder company which went into voluntary liquidation.

Although such starts were unexpected and unplanned, the successful companies proceeded to exploit the opportunities in a methodical and professional way.

Overcoming barriers to entry

Companies wishing to export have always faced huge barriers. Differences in language, culture, technical training, tariffs and government bureaucracy are just some of the obstacles faced. This is particularly true for UK firms and explains why many businesses historically have performed better by exporting to Commonwealth countries where the language, culture and legal systems are more familiar. In contrast, the USA and Europe have often been problem areas; the USA because while it appears similar it is culturally quite different, and Europe because of the language barrier and 'invisible' local protectionism.

It is generally considered that acquisition is a high risk option for a mid-size business. For example, Modiano and Ni-Chionna (1986), in their McKinsey study on export growth businesses, found that 'acquisition was the riskiest way to grow' and that 'well over half of their sample had not lived up to their hopes or expectations'. Despite this, only one of the five successful case study companies grew by setting up an entirely new operation in an overseas market. The remaining four grew by acquisition.

There was general agreement in our companies that acquisition was the route of least risk. Mid-size companies generally do not have the resources or depth of experience to enter a new market by the 'green-field' route. The director of the public relations company said that in his experience a 'start-up' takes twice as long and three times the cost of an acquisition before profitability is reached. Nevertheless, it was also agreed that considerable time and effort was needed in selecting and negotiating an acquisition, a subject dealt with in more detail later.

The senior executives of the businesses were well aware of the cultural, social and language barriers that existed and accepted that it would be risky for a British management team to run a foreign subsidiary. In order to overcome these barriers they sought to acquire a successful company with a skilled management team and with business philosophies and ethics similar to their own.

Usually they tried to acquire the market leaders in their equivalent foreign niches so that they would attract and retain the top clients and the best staff. By choosing the same niche they already understood the products and services, which again lowered the risk.

Another dimension considered in the choice of foreign market was the potential for growth. The chairman of the packaging and chemicals group said 'we get the information, no matter what the cost'. Similarly, the clothing company commissioned a 12-month study of the Japanese market, using a local consultant, prior to entering that market.

From a practical stand-point the companies took some time to identify a suitable target company for acquisition. They then took from nine months to two years researching and 'getting to know' the management of the potential acquisition. Not only did they examine financial and other conventional data, they researched customers, suppliers and other 'stakeholders'. Moreover, they were only prepared to deal with willing acquisition targets – no hostile takeovers were undertaken by our sample companies.

In the case of the 'unsuccessful' takeover the management thought that they had moved too quickly to buy a company which did not fit their overall company strategy. Also, whilst the business looked good on paper, they did not corroborate this with research into the customer base or the company's reputation with its suppliers. As a result, they bought a business which performed at nowhere near the expected level.

Building competitive advantage

These internationally successful businesses were usually able to strengthen their competitive advantages as a result of the acquisitions. The advantages arose either through economies of scale and reduced unit costs, or by being able to deliver a more comprehensive service for their international customers. A particularly important aspect emphasized at the interviews was the need to make the owners of the acquired subsidiaries feel that the change in ownership brought competitive benefits. This involved a 'courting' process taking a great deal of time. The director of the public relations group also confirmed that by close attention to this process they had been able to have a lower bid accepted through being the preferred acquirer.

Organizing for international supergrowth

The rapid growth rate of supergrowth businesses demands periodic restructuring of the organization. When an international dimension is added, further stress is put on the organization structure and we wished to discover how this was managed.

Because growth by acquisition is a lengthy and time-consuming business, the senior executives in the companies spent a great deal of time planning and negotiating acquisitions. They therefore had little time to devote to operational or service issues. As a result of this we found that the group boards spent time purely on strategic matters. For example, the public relations business had originally operated with five executive board members, but then changed so that the main board was compact and could concentrate solely on corporate development. The four directors involved in client services stepped down from the main board so that they too could focus on running the business.

The sales promotion business, which had problems, did not discover the time requirement for overseas expansion early enough and the managing director and his partner were attempting to manage both the international development and the domestic business. He said, 'the biggest mistake that we made was that we didn't bring in a senior management team to run the operations'.

The general pattern we found was that either one main board member was made responsible for international growth or the business was divided into international regions and responsibilities were allocated to a number of directors.

Controlling the international business

In all cases the foreign subsidiaries acquired were good performers employing skilled and competent management teams. This enabled those businesses to be run in a highly autonomous fashion. The main area for tight central control was finance.

The director of the public relations company outlined their philosophy:

It is important to allow these companies which are, after all well-managed and profitable, to keep their original management. The people have usually set up their own businesses and so they are entrepreneurs at heart and hence need that autonomy. They must retain their original culture but they must also develop a uniformity of reporting.

The monthly standardized reporting system used by the public relations company included:

- Cash flow forecasts
- Profit and loss and balance sheet results
- New business prospects
- Client billing
- Staff changes
- Debtor listings

It was common for targets to be set by consultation between the subsidiary management team and the group boards. In the computer services business, for example, an annual planning meeting is held at which the subsidiary heads agree five-year group objectives and a plan for the following 12 months. Each subsidiary produces its own detailed plan and, once agreed, this is used as the basis for quarterly reviews at which progress against the plan is monitored.

The parent company executives stressed the need for performance-linked reward systems with targets based on profits not sales.

Preparation for the single European market

At the time of the research the advent of the single European market in 1992 was being highly publicized. The response of the interviewees to this was that whilst they felt that it represented a general opportunity they could not be specific about any particular opportunity which it presented for their companies. They also felt that it had been a great deal overplayed, and that there was no need for them to take any specific steps to deal with it, over and above the plans they were already making for further international expansion. Similarly, none of the companies thought that the 1992 initiative would increase the need to protect their home markets, and they were not adopting any new defensive strategies to deal with it.

Doing your homework

At the end of each interview the executive was asked what was the biggest mistake to be avoided when trying to expand overseas. Without exception, the response was 'not doing your homework' on the market, the competition and the culture. Additionally, two executives said that underestimating the management time involved in setting up and carrying out international business was an important and often ignored factor. The business which had had problems with its overseas venture made both these mistakes, and the director interviewed commented that 'we became so enthusiastic about our venture that we seemed to forget the basic rules'.

While the sample size was small, the common nature of the experiences has confirmed the main factors leading to success in going international and highlighted some of the main obstacles that have to be overcome. Above all, the research emphasizes that to go international a company needs a single-minded 'champion' at the top of the business who will lead the process.

Building an international bridgehead

13

The results reported in this chapter are based on work carried out by George Laverty[1] on a sample from the database of 334 internationally orientated high-growth companies shown in Chapters 11 and 12. The purpose of this work, which was sponsored by Price Waterhouse, was to investigate the entry strategies used by the companies to penetrate overseas markets.

A report produced by Coopers and Lybrand in 1989[2] suggested that merger and acquisition was the primary strategy employed for international expansion. Their report also highlighted the problems experienced by British firms wishing to expand into other parts of the European Community. In general they found that Europe was simply not a 'level playing field' and many overt and hidden barriers existed which made expansion by acquisition or merger into many countries difficult to achieve and, where acquisitions did occur, they often failed. We therefore assumed that merger or acquisition would be the entry method chosen by most of the companies investigated.

The questions asked

The main questions asked were as follows:

- What internationalization strategies had these companies adopted?
- Which strategy had become the predominant one?
- What were the reasons for choosing their overseas markets?
- What problems or entry barriers did they experience with their main strategy?
- If acquisition was the major method, what were the key factors involved?

The survey results

Strategies for overseas expansion

Table 13.1 shows the expansion strategies chosen by the firms. As most of the companies used more than one method, the table is in two parts; the first shows all the methods used and the second the main method chosen.

Table 13.1 Method of international expansion.

Expansion method	One of several methods used		Main method used	
	Number of companies	*Per cent*	*Number of companies*	*Per cent*
1. Joint venture	6	30	2	10
2. Licensing	2	10	0	0
3. Acquisition and merger	15	75	13	65
4. Agents and distributors	11	55	3	15
5. Green-field	5	25	0	0
6. Acquisition of UK company	6	30	0	0
7. Collaboration	2	10	1	0
8. Franchise	1	5	1	5

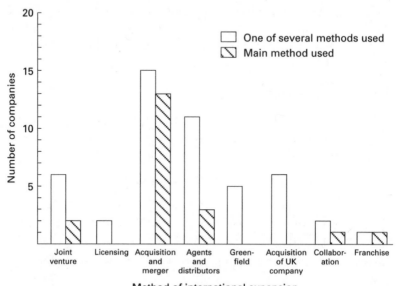

Method of international expansion

Figure 13.1

The results show two dominant strategies: *acquisition and mergers were used by 75 per cent of the companies, and agents and distributors by 55 per cent*. Some of the other methods, like franchising may suit particular sectors, but there is no general trend. It is interesting to note that although five of the businesses indicated that they used the 'green-field' approach – which is basically international expansion through organic growth – none had chosen this approach as a main strategy. *When it comes to choosing a main strategy, acquisitions and mergers dominates on its own as the choice of 65 per cent of businesses, with agents and distributors coming second at 15 per cent*. Also, a significant number of businesses (six) had gained overseas business through acquiring other UK businesses.

These results can be explained by the fact that the *use of agents and distributors is a popular initial strategy for taking the first steps into new markets*. It is a low-risk strategy and suitable for building initial business volume; it may then be superseded by an acquisition and merger strategy which is more suitable for long-term growth and more extensive market penetration, but requires heavy investment.

Number of methods used

Table 13.2 is an analysis of the number of methods used by the respondents. The range reflects the need to vary the expansion strategy according to factors such as the type of market, the level of risk incurred and the availability of suitable business partners.

Table 13.2 Number of methods used.

Number	Number of companies	Per cent
One expansion method	6	30
Two expansion methods	6	30
Three expansion methods	5	25
Four expansion methods	3	15
Total	20	

Relationship of expansion method with other factors

There was no obvious link between the entry strategies used by the sample companies and other factors such as industry type, country selection, or growth rate. The one significant observation was that only three (15 per cent) of the firms were service businesses compared with 214 (64 per cent) of the total database. This supports the view that services are more difficult to export than products.

Success ratings

The Coopers and Lybrand survey had suggested that many acquisitions and mergers had failed to deliver the results anticipated and were a disappointment to management. The responses of the chief executives to the question 'How successful has your main overseas expansion strategy been?' is shown in Table 13.3.

Table 13.3 Success rating of expansion methods.

	Rating				
Expansion method	Unsuccessful	Fairly successful	Successful	Very successful	Extremely successful
1. Joint venture				1	
2. Licensing					
3. Acquisition and merger			5	4	4
4. Agents and distributors	1		1	1	
5. Green-field					
6. Acquisition of UK company					
7. Collaboration				1	
8. Franchise		1			

The fact that no respondents admitted to being unsuccessful in their expansion strategy is interesting because it presents a direct contrast with the findings of the Coopers and Lybrand study. This sample was, of course, not representative of all businesses because only high-growth firms were included in the database and it is also possible that those firms which responded to the questionnaire were the more successful businesses. Nevertheless this does indicate that for many high-growth firms the acquisition and merger strategy was successful.

The main criteria for success as defined by the chief executives are shown in Table 13.4. *Although profitability is the major goal, competition for market share on a European or global scale is also a major consideration.*

Table 13.4 Criteria for success.

	Per cent
Profitability	58
Market-based goals	16
Competitor-orientated goals	5
Strategic goals	21

Choice of markets

The decision to enter a foreign market should be treated as an investment decision. Any such decision will require a considerable allocation of management time in addition to financial investments in purchasing a business and in providing marketing support, fixed assets and working capital. The attractiveness of a country will depend on its market potential, competitive situation and political and economic climate. Other factors like previous knowledge of trade in that market or the potential to serve the same customer groups as in the domestic market should also be considered.

An important choice factor is the wish to enter markets that are as close to the domestic market as possible so that successful products can be redeployed using the same or similar methods to those used in the home market.

The chief executives were asked to rate the importance of these factors using a scoring system. The results are shown in Tables 13.5 to 13.7. Table 13.5 shows the results for the whole sample, Table 13.6 shows the results from firms using acquisition and merger as the prime entry method, and Table 13.7 shows the results for those not using acquisition and merger as a main strategy.

Table 13.5 Importance rating scores for market selection criteria
(all entry methods).

Factor	*Importance rating*				
	Low 1	*2*	*3*	*4*	*5 High*
Growth potential	1	3	4	4	8
Level of competition	6	2	5	4	3
Previous experience	3	4	5	5	3
Geographic location	15	3	2	0	0
Similarity to UK	8	2	4	4	2
No product changes	9	4	3	2	2
Influence of UK clients	13	2	1	3	1
Same market/customers	1	1	5	6	7

Importance rating scores: 1 = Unimportant; 2 = Fairly important;
3 = Important; 4 = Very important; 5 = Extremely important.

Table 13.6 Importance rating scores for market selection criteria (for firms
using acquisition and mergers as their major entry strategy).

Factor	*Importance rating*				
	Low 1	*2*	*3*	*4*	*5 High*
Growth potential	1	1	2	3	6
Level of competition	5	0	4	2	2
Previous experience	3	0	3	4	3
Geographic location	10	1	2	0	0
Similarity to UK	3	2	3	3	2
No product changes	5	3	2	1	2
Influence of UK clients	8	1	1	2	1
Same market/customers	1	0	4	2	6

The highest rated factors for the whole sample were 'growth potential' and the ability to target similar well-defined markets and customers. The geographic location and the influence of UK clients were generally considered unimportant.

The firms using acquisition and merger as their main strategy also rated highly 'previous experience of the country'. This is not surprising because those involved in acquisition and merger are taking far more risk than those using third parties like agents and distributors who supply the country knowledge and

Table 13.7 Importance rating scores for market selection criteria (for firms where acquisition and mergers is not their major entry strategy).

	Importance rating				
Factor	*Low 1*	*2*	*3*	*4*	*5 High*
Growth potential	0	2	2	1	2
Level of competition	1	2	1	2	1
Previous experience	0	4	2	1	0
Geographic location	5	2	0	0	0
Similarity to UK	5	0	1	1	0
No product changes	4	1	1	1	0
Influence of UK clients	5	1	0	1	0
Same market/customers	0	1	1	4	1

take on much of the local risk themselves. For the same reason, another factor 'similarity to UK culture' is relatively unimportant for those *not* using non-acquisition and merger strategies, for instance, those using local agents or distributors.

Views on the 'level of competition' are fairly well divided. As these firms were often operating in niche markets in which competition was not strong, the aim was often to establish a presence quickly before competition developed.

Barriers to entry

Entrants to foreign markets face many barriers to entry. Mid-size companies, for example, typically do not have a large management structure, and the negotiations associated with overseas business can present a significant drain on management time. The chief executives were asked to identify major barriers from their own experience and score them according to their importance.

Tables 13.8 to 13.10 show the results for the whole sample (Table 13.8), for those using acquisition and merger as a main strategy (Table 13.9) and for the rest (Table 13.10).

From the results it seems that *the most significant barriers are the time constraints and the cultural issues.* The majority of companies surveyed found that the need to understand local customs and culture in depth presented a major barrier, particularly where acquisition and merger was their main entry strategy. Some of these companies also found that an absence

Table 13.8 Importance rating scores for barriers to entry (all entry methods).

	Importance rating				
Factor	*Low 1*	*2*	*3*	*4*	*5 High*
Time constraints	2	2	7	8	1
Experienced management	7	4	3	5	1
Language barriers	8	4	4	2	2
Market barriers	13	3	1	3	0
Tariff barriers	8	3	6	3	0
Technical barriers	11	5	2	0	2
Cultural barriers	1	3	5	7	4
Legal/bureaucracy problems	9	3	5	2	1

Importance rating scores: 1 = Unimportant; 2 = Fairly important;
3 = Important; 4 = Very important; 5 = Extremely important.

Table 13.9 Importance rating scores for barriers to entry (firms using acquisition and merger as their major entry strategy).

	Importance rating				
Factor	*Low 1*	*2*	*3*	*4*	*5 High*
Time constraints	1	0	5	6	1
Experienced management	5	1	2	4	1
Language barriers	4	2	4	1	2
Market barriers	7	2	1	3	0
Tariff barriers	7	2	2	2	0
Technical barriers	8	3	1	0	1
Cultural barriers	1	1	3	5	3
Legal/bureaucracy problems	6	3	2	1	1

of experienced management presented a barrier.

The companies which were not using acquisitions as their main strategy found tariffs and legal and bureaucracy problems more significant. This possibly results from the fact that they are shielded from many local difficulties by their trading partners which leaves the more technical areas as the major barriers.

Factors affecting expansion by acquisition

When questioned about the factors affecting expansion by acquisition, the items listed below were raised.

Table 13.10 Importance rating scores for barriers to entry (firms not using acquisition and merger as their major entry strategy).

Factor	Low 1	2	3	4	5 High
Time constraints	1	2	2	2	0
Experienced management	2	3	1	1	0
Language barriers	4	2	0	1	0
Market barriers	6	1	0	0	0
Tariff barriers	1	1	4	1	0
Technical barriers	3	2	1	0	1
Cultural barriers	0	2	2	2	1
Legal/bureaucracy problems	3	0	3	1	0

Company information

A sizeable minority (31 per cent) found it difficult to assess the real financial status of companies being acquired. In the USA, as in the UK, where many firms are publicly funded, company information is accessible and reliable, but in some continental countries, such as France and Italy where businesses tend to be private family firms, it is notoriously difficult to obtain accurate data.

Success of the target company

Eighty-five per cent of the sample said that they tried to acquire companies with a proven record of growth and success.

Rate of strategic development

All of the chief executives stated that they chose acquisition and merger as the fastest means of achieving international expansion.

Common products and markets

The firms chose acquisition and merger targets with common products and similar customers.

Common values

Seventy per cent of the sample felt that it was 'very' or 'extremely important' to acquire companies with similar ethics and business philosophy.

Acquiring market share

The chief executives were divided on the issue of whether to acquire market leaders in order to take a dominant position and to attract the best clientele and the best staff. Those settling for 'second best' may well not have had the funds or the reputation to acquire the leader.

Taking time to get to know the business

In almost all cases the chief executives confirmed the importance of investing time in getting to know the management and the business of the firm to be acquired.

Reporting structure

Seventy-seven per cent of chief executives said that they left the existing management in place to run the business, but imposed strict management reporting in order to provide overall control.

Size of the business to be acquired

Most companies acquired firms that were smaller than themselves, however 23 per cent felt that it was desirable to acquire companies of a similar size to themselves.

Conclusions

Although the sample size was small, the study indicates that high-growth firms use acquisition and merger as their main expansion strategy. The use of agents and distributors is also popular.

The *key factors for successful expansion* are:

- Enter niche markets which exhibit good potential for growth, and are relatively free of competition, by acting quickly.

- Stay with the same market and customer segments served in the domestic market.

- Invest a considerable amount of management time in studying the management, the country culture and the markets of the potential acquisitions.

- Where possible leave the existing management in place but impose strict financial controls.

- Acquire smaller businesses, but select companies which have demonstrated success and a record of growth in their own markets.

Notes

1 George Laverty (1990) *International Expansion Strategies Adopted by High-Growth Medium-Size UK Companies.*
2 Coopers and Lybrand (1989) *Barriers to Takeover in the EC*, HMSO.

Our final investigation on exporting supergrowth businesses concerned the ability to make service businesses international. Both the original study of mid-size high-growth companies and the second database compiled for the study of international expansion showed a predominance of service businesses. Yet the study reported in Chapter 13 showed that only 3 out of 20 respondents were from successful international service businesses. Given the importance of the service sector to the British economy it was decided to investigate the strategies leading to successful internationalization by mid-size high-growth companies and this study was carried out by Edward Mackenzie[1].

The research approach

The research addressed four main issues:

1. What are the differences between services and products when they are traded internationally?
2. What are the main factors to be considered when trading services internationally?
3. What are the key characteristics of successful international service businesses?
4. What are the strategies which they use for overseas expansion?

The concepts underlying the research questions

1 *What makes services more difficult to export than products?*

The first issue concerns the fundamental differences between services and products which affect the comparative portability and export potential. For example, it is far simpler to present a product to an overseas trading partner or customer than it is to present a service, as the purpose and use of most products is self-explanatory.

Professor Christian Grönroos's[2] work has indicated that there are five main elements that distinguish services from products:

- Services are transient – they have no lasting material presence.

- Services are mainly represented by people who form an important and integral part of the service as perceived by the customer.

- Services are made through personal contact and are consumed at the time of delivery. They are therefore 'instant and perishable' and cannot be stored for future demand.

- Services frequently constitute a series of 'one-off' production runs and therefore they are difficult to standardize and control.

- Services are often influenced by the customer since he or she participates in the activity.

The key point for overseas trade in services is that in the case of products the customer's perception of quality, fitness for purpose, and value for money is largely influenced by factors controlled at the centre like design and manufacturing performance. By contrast, *the customer's perception of service quality is largely determined by performance of individuals at the point of delivery which is much more difficult to control.* Service business strategy is therefore frequently aimed at 'productizing' services in order to improve the consistency of service delivery and to reduce the scope for local variations.

2 What key factors need to be considered when marketing services internationally?

Many of the factors leading to success in export markets will be the same as those employed to deliver a competitive edge in the domestic market. The factors dealt with here are those that specifically apply when marketing services internationally. For example Cowell[3] identifies three types of factors:

- the risks of international marketing for service organizations;
- the effect of different national social, cultural, economic and legal norms and the need to adapt services to fit them;
- barriers to trade in services.

The risks associated with service businesses tend to be greater than for manufacturers because a comprehensive approach is usually required to transfer the service package and the relevant management system overseas. By comparison a manufacturer is often able to test the product in the market through export agents with minimal risk.

The need to adapt to the local conditions without losing the core business values and the business concept are often summarized in the phrase 'Think global, act local'. Kenichi Ohmae[4] describes the ideal state of 'insiderization' where international firms are considered by customers and employees to be local despite the fact that they maintain a consistent international identity.

3 What are the characteristics of successful international service businesses?

Service businesses share many of the success factors that apply to all businesses. For example, competitive advantage arises from a close evaluation of customer needs, and the efficient application of technology, management and marketing techniques. According to Dunning[5] the following competitive advantages that arise from successful international operations also apply to service businesses:

1. *Quality and differentiation:* the provision of a high quality, differentiated service provides competitive advantage – however, the service provider must provide consistency of service.

2. *Economies of scope:* the price and availability of services depends upon the range of products offered by the seller. Outlets like retail stores can offer such economies, e.g. one-stop shopping.

3. *Economies of scale:* are more likely to be achieved with those services that are *reproducible*. Given the element of personal involvement in the delivery of many services, the scope for operational economies is often limited. Nevertheless, economies can be achieved in areas like marketing, service development, purchasing and so on.

4. *Knowledge and experience:* the provision of information about services delivery, markets, customers and employees when combined with experience can provide a core competitive advantage.

A report by Ken Irons, published by the Economist Intelligence Unit[6] on strategies for success in service businesses reported that 'services are relationships, successful services are successful relationships'. This emphasizes the need to adapt the service delivery to suit local customer needs. The report lists the following ingredients for success:

- There is a need for a strong 'service culture' with clear value delivered consistently.
- The customer must be the focus, and the relationship with the customer is the key to the customer's perception of service quality.
- Devolved power – a control framework is required which allows individuals to respond to varying customer demands as appropriate.
- A 'leadership style' should be employed that empowers individuals rather than enforces rigid central control.

To these should be added the factors identified by the previous Henley studies as leading to success in the high-growth midsize companies which were predominantly from the service sector:

- The deployment of niche marketing.
- Flexibility in response to changing customer needs and new market conditions.
- A focus on people and the ability to recruit and retain high-quality staff.
- The maintenance of high standards and values.

4 What strategies should be used for overseas expansion?

The previous studies highlight the most popular strategies employed for international expansion for both manufacturing and service businesses. They are:

- Expansion through the same foreign market niche as in the home market.
- Expansion through the same core products and services.
- Competition based on value rather than price.
- Expansion by acquisition to achieve economies of scale and instant local knowledge, targeting companies with a similar company culture.

The research was designed to test the relative importance of these factors in helping service businesses to penetrate international markets.

The research methodology

The database of 334 companies contained 64 companies that were service businesses operating both in the UK and abroad. The results here are based on general research into a sample of 25 of these businesses and detailed case studies prepared on five of them.

The sample of 25 companies derived between 20 per cent and 70 per cent of their total sales revenue from overseas. The proportion of foreign sales achieved by them is shown in Table 14.1. Over half of this group derived more than 30 per cent of sales from overseas.

Table 14.1 Proportion of overseas sales in the selected sample.

Percentage of sales	Number of companies
10–19	7
20–29	4
30–39	7
40–49	2
50–59	1
60–69	2
70–79	1
80–89	1
Total	25

The case study companies

The case study companies, which have to remain anonymous, provided significant variety in the nature of their businesses, as shown in Table 14.2; they also serve different types of customers.

Research results

The strategy for market entry

Although the earlier studies had identified acquisition and merger as the predominant foreign market entry strategy, the five case study companies used a wide range of entry strategies reflecting the different types of businesses involved. The

Table 14.2 Nature of the case study companies.

Company	Type of business	Type of customers
A	Buying and retailing	Individuals
B	Public relations	Individuals, businesses, public services and government
C	Automotive repair centres	Individuals and businesses
D	Business support services	Businesses and public services
E	Design and retailing	Individuals and businesses

public relations and business services companies chose *acquisition* as their market entry strategy because it offered the fastest route to establishing an international market position.

Both of the retailers used *franchising* as their preferred entry method. This not only permitted fast expansion but also required the minimum investment in resources and generated income from the selling of franchises. One of the retailers was also using other methods like equity *joint ventures* as well as setting up its *own outlets* where this was appropriate for the prevailing market conditions. Nevertheless both retailers viewed franchising as the best option, for the reasons given above and also as the best method for motivating success (due to the franchisee's financial commitment) and as the ideal way of replicating the success of their UK business. The very specific terms of the franchise agreements together with the strict enforcement of the terms, protects the parent company and ensures that service standards are uniformly applied, giving *consistent service delivery*.

The fifth company, with its chain of automotive repair centres, had set up its own branch network.

Four of the five companies stated that the most significant *barrier* to entering overseas markets was *the establishment of a market reputation*. They used their brand, their company reputation and their company values, to attract potential franchisees, customers or takeover targets according to their chosen strategy.

The type of service offered
In this instance all five companies showed a high degree of commonality of approach. In every case, *the same core service*

was also offered in their international markets. In the case of the business services company a reduced portfolio of services was offered with some ancillary services being held back. Very little adaptation was made to the services offered, although where companies were acquired the acquired business was already adapted to local conditions. All the companies held strong views about the type of business they were in and they strongly resisted any diversion from the core business. It was a case of 'stick to the knitting'.

In all cases, the international expansion was into the same market niches serving the *same types of customers*. The two companies offering business services were usually dealing with the same international clients in other geographic markets, i.e. moulding the service to the clients' international needs. These businesses were also developing a wider portfolio of services to meet more of the needs of these clients in a standard way around the world.

Company values and management system

All the companies displayed a *set of company aims and values* which were firmly placed at the core of the business. These really were more than just 'window dressing'. Many businesses these days can point to a mission statement, but few really show full commitment to the contents. All five businesses had strong, and quite distinctive values. One of the retailers displayed a 'charter' in all of its outlets at home and abroad, and the automotive repair centres displayed a code of practice that defines the level of service a customer should expect.

These values were firmly adhered to when internationalizing the business through:

- the training of personnel,
- care in the selection and recruitment of staff or business partners,
- the visibility and importance given to codes of practice, company charters and mission statements,
- and, in some instances, by carefully chosen acquisitions.

Above all, *the managers give visible and continuing support to the maintenance of standards through personal visits and frequent inspections*. The automotive service centres are

constantly monitored through the use of customer questionnaires and there is independent monitoring by the Automobile
Association.

Most of the companies had exported a *complete management
system*. International expansion simply involved reproducing
the UK system. Each involves service delivery through
branches together with strong central support and co-ordinated
activities like advertising, promotion, purchasing, warehousing
and control. The shared management system ensures consistency of standards and establishes a strong identity.

The basis for competition

All the businesses were agreed on the need to give customers
a uniformly *high quality of service*. This involved the quality of
the service itself and the perception of quality conveyed by the
delivery system. These form the main basis for competition.

None of the firms serving personal customers believed that
they were offering the cheapest price but all were convinced
that they offered best *value for money*.

The companies offering business services followed the same
route and believed that *by offering a perception of high quality,
individual attention and total professionalism, they were satis-
fying their clients and price was a secondary issue*. Their reputation for service quality was making them a preferred supplier
around the world, for a number of their major clients.

Three of the companies also stated that *low unit costs* were
important to their business because they enabled them to
deliver an excellent service at a reasonable price.

Personal contact

There was unanimity on the vital role of *personal contact* in
delivering services successfully. Both the companies serving
businesses emphasized that *personal attention was vital in
building and maintaining client relationships*. Two other
factors were important: 'getting it right first time' – there is
usually only one chance to get customer service right – and the
'one-off production run'. Business services often rely upon
different people to deliver individual elements of the overall
service transaction. This can be difficult to co-ordinate if the
service is being supplied simultaneously in different geographic locations.

The importance of the *customer relationship* is reflected in the strategy for internationalization of these businesses through:

- *A strong emphasis on training and education* which is conducted internally in company training centres to ensure that corporate values are reflected in all training.

- *Continuous monitoring of the relationship* both internally and by independent bodies together with great reliance placed upon local managers to deliver and maintain standards.

- *Empowerment of the employee to meet customer needs at the time of the service transaction.* The employee must operate within a framework of values but should not need to refer normal decisions back to higher authority for approval. One retailer said 'everyone who is part of the organization is taking an increased share in the responsibility for the day-to-day running of the business'.

Key factors for success

These have largely been covered explicitly or by implication in the previous sections:

- *Service culture* – The presence of a strong service culture was evident in all of these successful businesses, with an emphasis on a 'vision for service' and the practical delivery of consistent high quality.

- *Customer focus* – All five companies emphasized the importance of the relationship with customers, with particular attention to the factors that customers themselves perceive as being important. This view was reflected in the emphasis on training, selection of good-quality personnel, maintenance of service quality and professionalism.

- *Devolved power and visible leadership* – The need for devolved power was associated directly with the need to manage distributed operations effectively. The clear leadership style was demonstrated both by widespread communication of the value framework and the high-profile support of company values by the business leaders, i.e. leadership by example.

Other findings

A major factor which enables services to be marketed overseas is *the ability to package or 'productize' services*. One of the best examples of this is provided by the businesses using a franchise strategy. *In order to sell a franchise, the whole service concept has to be specified and packaged in great detail so that the franchisee can replicate the service in all respects.* At the same time the franchisor wants to ensure that the world wide image is totally consistent so that the whole wider 'family' of outlets presents a consistent image and a similar service is delivered around the world. It is only by planning the package in great detail that the service delivery can be maintained and controlled.

The companies which were interviewed employed a number of mechanisms that helped them maintain consistency of service as the business expanded. These were:

- *A strong brand and company image in the home market* – perhaps one of the best examples of this in the service sector is demonstrated by McDonald's, the fast food chain.

- *The training of employees, managers, franchisees, business partners* and anyone else involved in corporate systems and values, coupled with the devolution of power and responsibility to people in contact with the customers.

- *The embodiment of principles, values and detailed working practices in franchising agreements.*

- *Company staff themselves working with suppliers* to encourage consistent service provision in all key markets.

- *The development of an international team of employees,* who can assure quality and monitor the consistency of approach in the different international markets and help to deliver the service.

In general the businesses had made remarkably little effort to customize the services to the local markets. Their major selling point was the strength and consistency of the brand which might be diluted or lose some of its differentiation by adaptation. The one exception to this was the PR company, which encouraged its acquired subsidiaries to be specifically local. This is not surprising given the need to adapt public relations to local social and political conditions.

One other common observation was the reliance placed by all the companies on *computerized information systems.* For example, the use of electronic point of sale (EPOS) systems by one retailer provided rapid information on sales, margins and stock levels. This was a major contributor to cost competitiveness and permitted close control of their widely dispersed branches.

Conclusion

Although the final sample was small, and varied in their international development strategies, there is close agreement on the factors which their top managers believe lead to success. All the businesses were very successful and each had its own formula for success. There are a number of factors that seem to apply to all service businesses. *Service businesses that lend themselves to being 'packaged' seem to be better able to expand overseas than those which offer more diffuse or varied services.* Nevertheless there are a number of excellent role models here for any service business contemplating foreign expansion.

Notes

1 Edward A. Mackenzie (1992) *International Strategies for Service Businesses*. Henley Management College.
2 Based on work by Professor Christian Grönroos, Svenska Handelshogskolan, Helsinki.
3 Cowell, D.W. (1983) International Marketing of Services. *The Service Industries Journal*, **3**, No 3.
4 Ohmae, K. (1987) Planting for a Global Harvest. *Harvard Business Review*, March-April.
5 Dunning, J.H. (1989) Multinational Enterprises and the Growth of Services: Some Conceptual and Theoretical Issues. *The Service Industries Journal*, **9**, No. 1.
6 Irons, K. (1991) *Managing Service Companies: Strategies for Success*, The Economist Intelligence Unit, Management Guides.

Part 4
Summarizing the results

In this final chapter we attempt to pull together the understanding we have gained from the various studies undertaken at Henley and to draw the overall conclusions on the key common factors that lead to success for this important class of businesses.

Chapter 15
Conclusion – the role and dynamics of supergrowth businesses.

Conclusion – the role and dynamics of supergrowth businesses   15

The various research studies contained in this book have led us to a series of conclusions about the characteristics of supergrowth businesses, the key role they play in the economy of a country and the critical factors that contribute to their successful growth.

The distinctive characteristics of supergrowth companies

An initial hypothesis that we confirmed was that the supergrowth businesses represent a discrete group of businesses in the UK with a role analogous to that demonstrated in the USA by parallel research studies. Our criteria could have produced a collection of firms distinguished only by their size and growth rate without other unique features to separate them from the usual run of businesses. On the one hand, we were looking for characteristics which distinguished them from the majority of small- and medium-sized enterprises, on the the other hand we expected them to be clearly differentiated from the general run of large businesses.

As a result of our research we were able to develop a business growth model based on the size of the businesses but also differentiated by quite separate characteristics across a common set of criteria. Figure 15.1 shows how the various stages of growth are typically characterized by differences in leadership, leadership skills, business scope, organization, control systems and barriers to growth.

In addition to the differences in size, the extraordinary growth rate which the businesses achieved was also associated with unusual characteristics. These are required because of the management challenges faced by supergrowth businesses. The average manager would find it difficult, or even impossible, to cope with the constant challenges and changes that occur when a business is growing at some 40 per cent per annum – doubling in size every two years – as many of our featured

Stages

Characteristics	1	2	3	4
Size	Small	Mid-size	Large national	Large international
Leader	One-man band	Professional entrepreneur	Corporate leader	International leader
Leadership skills	Entrepreneurial	plus Organization/ delegation	plus External communication	plus International communication
Business scope	Single business	Limited diversification	Diversified business	Multinational
Organization	Functional	Business units	Divisions	Divisions and regions
Control systems	Informal	Simple ratios	Formal systems	International systems
Key barriers	Funding Market development Skilled people	New products New markets Professional managers	Public funding Market development New technologies	International markets Legal and cultural Funding/partners

Figure 15.1 Key characteristics of the growth stages in high-growth businesses. © Taylor, Harrison and Tampoe.

companies have done. The tasks of finding additional skilled people and the necessary financial support represent major hurdles in addition to the job of dealing with a rapidly expanding customer base.

Some companies do not pass the test. Acorn – one of the first companies studied – failed to capitalize on its early success with the BBC computer and was only saved from total collapse by Olivetti. The management were trying to cope with growth rates of 70–80 per cent per annum, and the business ran out of control.

Of course small businesses often realize similar growth rates, but they do not have to manage the scale, and the complexity, that medium-sized businesses face. The additional complexity is often caused by the need to expand geographically and to manage operations remote from the home base, a challenge which the small local business does not face.

At the other end of the scale, few large businesses can sustain the kind of annual growth rate demonstrated by the supergrowth companies – on average 40–50 per cent. Those which do, like Hewlett Packard, have often managed to nurture and retain many of the characteristics of the medium-sized high-growth business within their corporate framework. As many of the supergrowth companies end up as divisions of multi-national corporations, some of our future research studies will examine the characteristics of successful supergrowth divisions.

> There certainly is a discrete group of supergrowth companies with their own common characteristics for success.

The transient nature of the supergrowth business

Supergrowth, as we have defined it, can never be a permanent state. The companies simply pass through a stage in which they achieve high growth rates before they either become large high-growth businesses, or they slow down. Alternatively they may lose their independent status through being merged with or acquired by a larger business.

The businesses come from a variety of backgrounds. They may originate as small businesses, as declining or dormant mid-size businesses, or as businesses which emerge ready-made from a privatization, or a management buy-out. They enter the supergrowth phase usually through exploiting a 'window of business opportunity'. Then, in the supergrowth phase, they grow rapidly.

This rapid growth phase can last for 12 to 15 years, by which time the businesses have become substantial large businesses. Virgin, Kwikfit and Laura Ashley are typical examples of this type of business. Many more businesses do not last long, either as independent businesses, or with their original management teams because:

- *They represent attractive takeover targets* for larger industry competitors, as Underwoods retail chemists did for Boots and Derwent Foods did for United Biscuits.

- *Their industry undergoes a period of concentration* into a few large companies, as did the publishing industry in the 1980s, which resulted in a significant number of supergrowth businesses being acquired.

- *The management makes an expensive mistake,* or fails to live up to the expectations of their backers (the City these days appears to be unforgiving in either event) and are replaced, as happened with Owners Abroad and Stakis.

- *Management becomes tired of the constant challenges* faced by a high-growth company in an uncertain business environment and they 'take the money'. This is often combined with one of the other factors. Tallent Engineering and Derwent Foods are typical examples of this situation.

A third group of businesses simply stagnate or decline as their 'window' of market opportunity runs out or they simply lose momentum as they fail to surmount one or more of the growth barriers. The voracious appetite of growth businesses for additional working capital often provides the greatest stumbling block. A business like Amstrad which was a star supergrowth company in the early 1980s has exploited a series of market niches. It has brought a succession of budget-priced, high-volume electronic products to domestic and business customers, including hi-fis, PCs, fax machines and satellite TV aerials, but the management has had to 're-invent the business' every few years to maintain its position.

Conclusion – the role and dynamics of supergrowth businesses

The important contribution of the supergrowth business

Supergrowth companies play a vital and special role in a capitalist economy and they bring significant benefits to society and to the business world.

Supergrowth companies' contributions to the economy:

- they produce wealth for entrepreneurs, investors and, frequently, management teams;
- they create jobs at a significant rate, and
- they are champions of innovation.

They form a bridge between the business start-ups, which form a central strategy of many governments' regeneration programmes, and the major established businesses, which often grow by acquisition.

For large businesses, the supergrowth companies are major developers of new ideas, new technologies and processes. They pioneer new products, new distribution systems and new markets. Their role is to take the ideas of inventors, designers and technologists, some of which will have been developed on a small scale, and turn them into mass-produced, mass-marketed products and services. Sometimes they lead the development of an entire industry, as was the case with British publishing.

The British publishing industry represents a case study in which a whole industry has been transformed through contributions by a number of supergrowth businesses. Publishers such as Hamlyn and Heinemann were small entrepreneurial businesses which – through exploiting the capabilities of new publishing technologies – were able to develop a world market for British books of all kinds, including management and reference books. Companies like Dorling Kindersley have continued the process of innovation in both products – their development of CD-Rom-based material has led to Microsoft making an investment in them – and in marketing (including direct selling through an agency/distributor structure).

Like many industries which have undergone such a period of development, the growth in profitability of the publishing

The vanishing independence

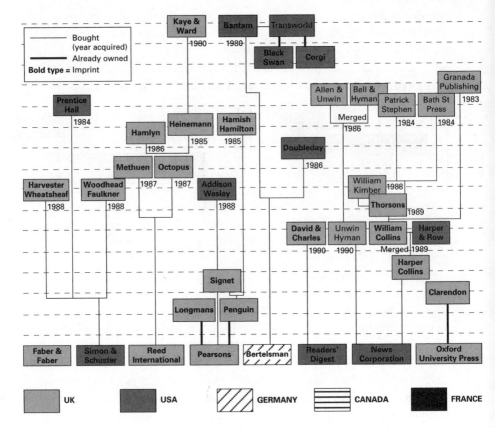

Figure 15.2 The rise of large companies in British publishing. Source: *The Independent,* 16 April 1995.

industry has resulted in considerable concentration through takeover. Figure 15.2 shows how this concentration has taken place.

Dynamics of the supergrowth company – the leadership role of the entrepreneur

The support given to small businesses tends to focus on supporting 'the entrepreneur'. Typical entrepreneurs who people think ofinclude Richard Branson, Anita Roddick and Alan Sugar. These are highly visible, self-made, individuals, driven by a vision and possessing a powerful charismatic personality and drive. Our research showed that this type of entrepreneur

of British publishing

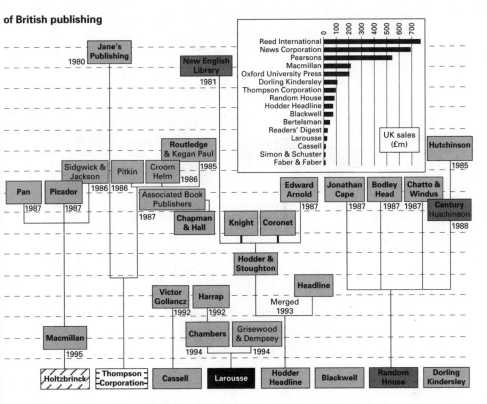

represents a minority of leaders in supergrowth businesses.

The typical leader was much more likely to be a professional manager, with large company experience, who had decided that they were likely to be happier and more successful running their own businesses. They had a clear vision, and the ability to communicate it, but they were not 'boot-strap entrepreneurs'. Their large company training and experience meant they were often better versed in marketing and financial management than the self-made person, and they tended to rely more on analysis than instinct. Thus Bill Cross, the founder of Brent International, was a former marketing director of Diversey, who having been passed over for the managing director's job, struck out on his own.

Another typical example was provided by Tim Waterstone who developed the chain of bookstores carrying his name. At the same time that the publishing trade was developing as outlined above, the retail book trade underwent a similar change with entrepreneurs like Tim Waterstone creating a new concept in book retailing. This involved the setting up of new large stores in prime sites, open at convenient times for working people, offering an environment suited to browsing and supported by knowledgeable staff. He was well trained in business management by a large company, WH Smith, which he left in order to pursue his vision of a different type of book shop. Ironically, his business was subsequently sold to WH Smith for a substantial sum.

> The key to supergrowth business leadership appears to be a blend of the vision and drive of the true entrepreneur, with the business skills and mentality of the professional manager.

The vision provides the blueprint for the business and its route to the 'window of opportunity' and the drive delivers the impetus to overcome any barriers that stand in the way.

At the same time the professional management skills provide the means to handle rapid business growth such as:

- *the ability to maintain the tight financial control* that is needed as a supplier to a multiple retailer such as Marks and Spencer, Sainsbury's or B&Q, and knowledge of how technology like EDI (electronic data interchange) can be introduced;

- *knowing how to delegate successfully* when developing additional product lines or penetrating new and remote markets;

- *knowing how to deal with financial institutions* when seeking additional funds;

- *the commercial approach to use when dealing with large international customers.*

Many of the businesses made the successful transition from a 'one-man band' through a functional organization then through a multi-divisional business to become a fully international organization. This process can only be accomplished if the senior managers are capable of learning fast and can build a team. Brent Chemicals International typifies this style.

Lessons from the recession of the early 1990s

> The recession that began to bite hard in 1991 really tested those leaders of supergrowth businesses who did not have clear sense of direction and a prudent financial strategy.

The weaknesses which became particularly apparent were:

- *The lack of a financial strategy to deal with the additional pressures caused by the recession.* Owners Abroad, for example, survived in the travel business when many others failed because its management had decided not to fund the business with borrowings.

- *The lack of a well-defined product/market focus, and a failure to understand the management's limitations.* John Ashworth at Coloroll believed that the formula which he had applied successfully in the wallpaper business could, just as easily, be applied to other areas of decoration, and then into soft furnishings. This expansion ultimately led to the business's downfall. Similarly, Reo Stakis went with considerable success from selling lace into the management of pubs and hotels suitable for families. But subsequent diversification into property development, casinos and financial services took the business away from the core areas of the management's competence and led to a crisis in confidence in the group's investors.

- *The failure to counter-balance the views of the leader.* The leader's views naturally tend to predominate, but, particularly when the business has been successful, the leader tends to back his or her judgement and to ignore the ideas and opinions of others. Most entrepreneurs need a partner – frequently someone who is more thoughtful and more introverted – who the leader respects and who can curb their wilder and more fanciful ideas. Bill Rooney, the head of Spring Ram, had a financial director who acted in such a role. When the financial director departed the counter-balance role was left vacant and the company started to get into trouble when it departed from its core expertise in kitchen and bathroom furniture into reproduction furniture and furniture retailing.

The characteristics of the entrepreneur and the 'partner'

> What we see in a typical successful business is a balance between the entrepreneur and a 'controller', or the deal maker and the manager.

The partner may be the chairman, the financial director, a non-executive director or may operate in some other executive role.

The entrepreneur is usually extrovert, highly creative, opportunistic, acts quickly, and lives in a world of great potential. By contrast the 'controller' has the complementary attributes of keeping financial control and managing the administration and he or she is frequently required to implement the decisions (and sometimes clean up the mess!) resulting from the entrepreneur's forceful leadership.

Another reason for this dual arrangement is the need for the leader to maintain strong links with customers, the marketplace and suppliers, i.e. to be a committed **outside person**. This means there is a clear need for an **insider** to deal with day-to-day issues within the business.

Barriers to market entry and growth

> A wide range of strategies is used by supergrowth businesses in order to overcome the barriers to market entry and subsequent growth.

Some supergrowth companies grow rapidly through doing business with a limited number of major customers. Many of the companies featured in the German study were manufacturing businesses which grew rapidly on the coat-tails of their customers (major German manufacturers like Daimler-Benz and BMW), through delivering innovative high-technology products. In the UK, this was a less common pattern, however Tallent Engineering, now a major producer of car chassis, was built through the development of close relationships with motor manufacturers like Rover, Ford and Nissan.

A more common route to high growth in Britain was to become a supplier to one of the large multiple retailers and capitalize on their growth. Businesses without an existing product reputation could develop sales rapidly as a *private label supplier* providing they could match the stringent service requirements demanded by the retail chains. The technological content of the product was often less important than that of the order, production and delivery process. The British supergrowth companies included suppliers of garments to Marks and Spencer, suppliers of fresh foods to the grocery multiples and suppliers of DIY products to chains like B&Q and Texas Homecare.

A frequent problem for these suppliers is that they become too dependent on a small number of customers, who usually are not prepared to enter into long-term contracts. This vulnerability can sometimes be reduced through a widening of the customer base, or as in the case of the Ring Group – a supplier of lighting kits to the DIY store chains – by developing a strong company brand and selling through a variety of distribution channels.

Another route to rapid growth was through vertical integration. Owners Abroad, for example, extended its flight booking operation into airline operations at one end of the business and by buying into travel retailing at the other end.

Niche marketing strategies

Another strategy for growth is through identifying a growing market niche and then using the company's skills and abilities to create an 'unfair advantage'. This advantage is typically gained through flexible service to customers and a quick response to orders. Many of the companies provided a higher level of service than their traditionally-based competitors.

A niche that has offered a continuing source of market opportunities has been the *out-sourcing of management services* in both commercial businesses that have shed 'non-core' activities and the 'externalization' of many public-sector services under the impetus of the government's campaign to encourage public sector organizations to adopt compulsory competitive tendering (CCT).

These new business opportunities have included market research, cleaning, waste disposal, security services, management consultancy, transport, logistics, information systems, estate management and staff training.

Sometimes companies have developed as a result of *a new product idea*. Derwent Foods identified a gap in the snack foods market which it addressed with its exotic Phileas Fogg range. Dyson has developed rapidly as a result of the founder's development of the concept of a 'dual cyclone' vacuum cleaner, which requires no dust bag.

A major barrier to the development of sales occurs when competition enters the niche. A number of mid-size businesses in our sample ceased growing when their core business matured. They then gained a new lease of life through the injection of a new management team, with fresh ideas. The Economist Group, for example, capitalized on its reputation in financial journalism by extending its overseas markets and adding new brands such as the Intelligence Unit and a series of Economist Books to its core magazine product. Similarly, Blackwells, the long-established Oxford bookshop, added additional branches and diversified into publishing international journals and books using its network of academic contacts as the basis of this expansion.

> The rule for success seems to be that companies should only diversify into related businesses.

It is clearly difficult to define the precise stage at which a diversification becomes 'unrelated'. The capacity for the company to extend its operations often depends on the capabilities of its management and skills of its staff and the attraction of the extension to the existing customer base.

Gaining access to technology

> One of the problems for the supergrowth company is how to gain access to the latest technology despite being relatively small as a user of technology. The usual route seems to be through partnership.

The following were typical examples:

• Spring Ram gained access to the latest *acrylic bath technology* through its close contacts with ICI.

- Celltech continued to maintain its technological development by maintaining close links with the *biotechnology* laboratories supported by the Medical Research Council and through British Universities.

- Iceland Foods employed existing *barcode technology* in order to provide systems for managing remote stores with the minimum of direct management supervision.

The special problems of supergrowth businesses in Britain

> Britain's supergrowth businesses have faced special problems compared with their European counterparts.

One problem has been the roller-coaster economy with the alternative boom and bust phases. The unpredictability of government policy tends to heighten the level of uncertainty. In some other parts of Europe the proportional representation voting system tends to result in coalition governments with far less ability to introduce radical changes which has tended to dampen the economic swings. *The temptation in the UK is therefore to make profits rapidly and opportunistically and to sell out before the next recession arrives.*

Britain, with its emphasis on the market economy, has also become *one of the most competitive markets in Europe*. There is free access to the UK market for overseas competition – a situation that is not always reciprocated in mainland Europe where more protectionism exists of one kind or another. The UK airline, banking and telecommunications markets have been opened up to competition ahead of most of their international counterparts.

Britain's companies therefore faced the myth of 1992 – for many businesses the single European market simply did not occur. Companies wishing to grow in mainland Europe face resistance from local banks and national banks with local interests embedded in the community – *the level playing field simply does not exist.*

The UK market economy also extends to selling the companies themselves. The UK, like the USA operates *an active market in companies*. The UK stock market is the largest in the world on a comparative basis. A much higher proportion of medium-sized UK businesses are funded by shares compared with mainland Europe where banks form a much more central role in company funding.

The *venture capital business* in the UK also puts pressure on companies to make money rapidly. The pressure for short-term results from the financial institutions has caused a number of companies such as the Really Useful Group to buy back their shares in order that management can take a longer-term view.

In many European countries it is still possible to have a small investment in a business with *a large voting share*. In some countries, like Switzerland, legislation remains in place which effectively prevents companies from being taken over. This means that many of the companies with pan-European ambitions through developing in the same niche overseas have been unable to realize their ambitions. The only market where these companies have tended to be successful is in America where a similar market for businesses exists.

Success in international markets

> Despite the barriers to international expansion, a number of our sample companies developed significant overseas businesses.

The Body Shop and Kwikfit have developed substantial overseas businesses based on a strategy of franchising which avoids the need to acquire overseas businesses. Brent International has concentrated on markets with international potential and, in many cases, on multinational customers with similar needs in a number of countries. Shandwick, the PR company, has also created a widespread international network of businesses and although it suffered setbacks in the recession of the early 1990s has now regained much of its former momentum.

The music industry has been a successful international area for British entrepreneurs, although some segments of this market have undergone rapid concentration, for example EMI is now the only sizeable UK producer of tapes and CDs.

One of the problems for the many British service-sector companies wishing to expand is that the service sector is responsible for only one third of UK overseas trade. Some businesses like Ford dealerships are specifically excluded from expanding overseas by the terms of their dealership agreements. However, in general it is much harder to export services than products because of the human side of service businesses. There are a number of services businesses that have become successful on a global basis. These include American Express, McDonald's, Benetton, Visa, Mastercard and WPP.

Industry concentration

The industry concentration demonstrated earlier in the publishing industry has been repeated in a number of other industries. These include the hotel, brewing and holiday industries. A number of privatized and deregulated industries are starting to show similar trends, with companies like Stagecoach taking a significant share of the bus transportation market, and a number of mergers and takeovers of utility companies being proposed at the time of writing.

This concentration is being driven by the economies of scale in production and the increased marketing power derived by larger businesses.

Key strategies for survival and growth

Throughout the research studies certain strategies have emerged as being important contributors to success in both boom and recession. These form action points for any aspirant supergrowth business manager:

- *Growing your people* The managers of fast growing businesses, both in small independent businesses and large groups, acknowledge that continually developing your people is a key strategy. This particularly applies to the people at the top of the organization who are continually facing new challenges as the business doubles in size every two to three years and then redoubles. They are therefore almost continuously short of leaders, skilled people and energetic and flexible people who can support the demands of supergrowth.

- *Having a clear strategic vision* This tells people what business they are in and *what they are not in*. It is particularly important that the factors that enable the business to compete are also clearly defined. Typical factors are:

– being able to respond quickly to customer demands
– focusing on a niche
– delivering first class service

Many of the firms studied competed well because they were recognised leaders in a market niche and were able to respond quickly and with flexibility when their larger rivals were slow and constrained in their responses. This was particularly evident in firms that were supplying own-brands to supermarket chains where excellent and quick response provides ready access to instant large market volumes.

- *Piggy-backing on a large company* Organic growth is hard for a medium-sized business to sustain when the growth demands rapid doubling and re-doubling of the customer base. By contrast, a symbiotic relationship with a larger partner, who is in turn generating significant growth, allows the firm to 'piggy back' on the growth curve. There were many examples of this type of relationship in the supergrowth businesses. The suppliers of supermarkets were one group of such businesses which had become an integral part of their customers' supply and distribution chains; others like Tallent Engineering and many of the German companies enjoyed a close relationship with one or more large manufacturing businesses.

- *Competing on quality and innovation, not on price* Although being the lowest-cost producer is an ideal position, it tends not to form a lasting basis for a sustainable strategy. Bill Cross at Brent International deliberately took the business away from the commodity chemicals sector, where the big competitors compete on price, to special niches where quality of service (dependability and reliability), innovation and value for money counted for more than absolute price. In many cases, those firms working with larger partners were playing an active part in designing new products and services for their customers, and were effectively acting as an extended part of their research and development department. One major large firm which still acts like a supergrowth business, 3M, claims that 30 per cent of its business comes from products that did not exist five years ago – its rationale for a commitment to constant innovation.

- *Having a financial strategy*   The rapid development of supergrowth companies tends to generate an insatiable appetite for cash resources. These need to be planned for so that the business has financial resources in place before they are needed and the business is forced to accept expensive emergency funding negotiated from a position of weakness. The periodic recessions put additional pressure on financial resources as growth tends to slow and fail to generate sufficient cash to cover committed investment plans. Those businesses that continue to thrive on an independent basis tend to do so through adopting a prudent financial strategy:

  - avoiding too much debt capital – funding growth through retained earnings, equity, or venture capital;
  - also avoiding the temptation to raise funds against inflated property values.

  We have also seen some firms resume a private funding position in order to avoid the short-term pressures imposed by financial institutions and enable them to concentrate on pursuing longer-term goals – only certain businesses can afford this route!

- *Maintaining an 'unfair advantage'*   To keep a supergrowth company growing it is necessary to maintain some 'unfair advantage' over competition. This may be through some formal barrier such as product patent protection or a special licensing arrangement. It may also occur through some unique access to technology or a special image; the Body Shop, although it has a number of me-too competitors, is still regarded as the definitive supplier in its market. In a number of other cases this barrier has been achieved through developing a close and binding relationship with one or more major customers. This relationship may not just be with a customer, it may be with some organization for mutual benefit. For example, Henley Management College, by allying itself with Brunel University, was the first independent management college able to award degrees.

- *Having an exit strategy* As many of the supergrowth firms are built on specialization within a particular niche, it is important to have an exit strategy as sooner or later the niche runs out. In some cases, as with Derwent Foods with their Phileas Fogg range, the niche became large enough to attract the mainstream competitors, and the owners allowed the business to be sold. In some cases the business will wish to continue to expand in recognized areas of opportunity:

  – in the same niche in overseas markets, or
  – in allied niches in the domestic market

In addition to Derwent Foods, a number of the supergrowth businesses did allow themselves to be sold for various reasons:

  – The owners of Robert Horne, the paper merchant, planned the sale of the business to one of the Scandinavian paper conglomerates when they recognized that the continuing vertical integration of the industry would make it increasingly difficult for them to compete.
  – Business Intelligence Systems sold themselves to Nynex when they recognised that they did not have the financial resources to fund their next stage of growth.

Because of the risks associated with high growth, the owners of supergrowth businesses will often be tempted to sell-out and restore their personal financial security, as the management buy-out team at Tallent Engineering have done. In some cases it is possible to make the leap from being a supergrowth business to a large, established business – from a niche player to a volume supplier. This tends to happen in high-technology businesses where business growth can be extremely rapid, and firms like Compaq can move from being a niche player to a major corporation in a few years. A UK business which is heading in a similar direction is Psion, maker of 'palmtop' computers which was valued at £3 million when launched on the stock market in 1988, and by September 1995 was valued at £122 million.

Whatever strategy is adopted, the world of the supergrowth business remains an exciting and volatile one where the top team need to show constant vigilance, boundless energy and considerable flexibility, matched with clarity of vision and purpose.

Areas for future research

As with many research-based projects, our studies have raised a number of additional questions that would form subjects for future research. These include: What are the success factors in medium-sized high-growth subsidiaries of large firms? Is intrapreneurship a myth? Can managers of subsidiaries of large businesses act as entrepreneurs? How do large companies like Mars, 3M and Hewlett Packard sustain their continuing level of innovation over many decades?

Bibliography

Albach, H., Bock, K. and Warnke, T. (1985) *Kritische Wachstumsschwellen in der Unternehmungsentwicklung.* In H. Albach and Hax (eds) Schriften zur Mittelstandsforschung, No. 7, Stuttgart, p. 145.

Anderson, E. and Gatignon, H. (1986) Modes of Foreign Entry: A Transaction Cost Analysis and Propositions, *Journal of International Business Studies,* **17** (3), 1–26.

Arbose, J. (1986) Expansion Abroad: The New Direction for European Firms. *International Management,* **41**, November, pp. 22–31.

Baden-Fuller, C. and Stopford, J.M. (1992) *Rejuvenating the Mature Business,* Routledge.

Bamberger, I. (1983) Value Systems, Strategies and Performance of Small and Medium-Sized Firms. *European Small Business Journal,* **1**, No. 4, Summer.

Buhner, R. (1987) Assessing International Diversification of West German Corporations. *Strategic Management Journal,* **8**, pp. 25–37.

Christiansen, C.H., da Rocha, A. and Gertner, R.K. (1987) An Empirical Investigation of the Factors Influencing Exporting Success. *Journal of International Business Studies,* **18**, Fall, pp. 61–77.

Churchill, N. and Lewis, V. (1983) The Five Stages of Small Business Growth. *Harvard Business Review,* May–June.

Clifford, D.K. (1973) Growth Pains of the Threshold Company. *Harvard Business Review,* September, pp. 143–54.

Clifford, D.K. and Cavanagh, R.E. (1985) *The Winning Performance.* Sidgwick and Jackson, London.

Clutterbuck, D. and Crainer, S. (1988) *The Decline and Rise of British Industry.* W.H. Allen.

Coopers and Lybrand (1989), *Barriers to Takeover in the EC.* Report for the Department of Trade and Industry, HMSO, London.

Coulson-Thomas, C. (1993) *Creating Excellence in the Boardroom.* McGraw-Hill, Maidenhead.

Cowell, D.W. (1983) International Marketing of Services. *The Service Industries Journal,* **3**, No. 3.

Curran, J. (1986) *Bolton Fifteen Years On.* Small Business Research Trust, London.

Deal, T. and Kennedy, A. (1982) *Corporate Cultures: The Rites and Rituals of Corporate Life,* Addison-Wesley, Reading, MA.

Devlin, G. and Bleakley, M. (1988) Strategic Alliances. *Long Range Planning,* **21**, No. 5, pp. 18–23.

Dickson, M. (1986) What Top Managers Think They Are Paid To Do. *Financial Times,* 24 April, p. 17.

Drucker, P.F. (1970) Entrepreneurship in Business Enterprise. *Journal of Business Policy,* **1** (1), Autumn.

Drucker, P.F. (1985) *Innovation and Entrepreneurship.* Butterworth–Heinemann, Oxford.

Dudley, J.W. (1989) *1992 – Strategies for the Single Market.* Kogan Page.

Dunning, J.H. (1989) Multinational Enterprises and the Growth of Services: Some Conceptual and Theoretical Issues. *The Service Industries Journal,* **9**, No. 1.

Foster, R. (1986) *Innovation: The Attacker's Advantage.* Macmillan, London.

Franck, G. (1990) Mergers and Acquisitions: Competitive Advantage and Cultural Fit. *European Management Journal*, **8**, No. 1, March.

Ghenawat, P. (1991) *Commitment: The Dynamic of Strategy*. Free Press.

Gluck, F.W. (1985) A Fresh Look at Strategic Management. *The Journal of Business Strategy*, Autumn, p. 5.

Goldston, M.R. (1992) *The Turnaround Prescription: Re-positioning Troubled Companies*. Free Press, New York.

Gomez-Meja, L.R. (1988) The Role of Human Resources Strategy in Export Performance. *Strategic Management Journal*, **9**.

Greiner, L.E. (1972) Evolution and Revolution as Organisations Grow, *Harvard Business Review*, **50** (4), July–August, p. 37.

Hahn, D. and Gräb, U. (1987) *West German High-Growth Medium-Size Companies*. University of Giessen study. Anglo-German Foundation.

Hartmann, H. (1971) Authority and Organisation in German Management. In S.M. Davis (ed.) *A Study of Comparative Management*. Prentice Hall, Englewood Cliffs, p. 407.

Henzler, H. and Rall, W. (1986) Facing up to the Globalisation Challenge. *The McKinsey Quarterly*, Winter.

Herbect, P. and Taylor, B. (1990) *International Strategies of Growing Companies*. Henley Management College/Price Waterhouse.

Heskett, J.L. (1986) *Managing in the Service Economy*. Harvard Business School Press.

Hitt, M.A. and Ireland, R.D. (1987) Building Competitive Strength in International Markets. *Long Range Planning*, **20**, No. 1, pp.115–22.

Hofstede, G. (1989) Organising for Cultural Diversity. *European Management Journal*, **7**, No. 4.

Houlden, B.T. (1992) *The Buy-Out Path to Successful Long Term Company Ownership*. Touche Ross, London.

Hutton, J. (1988) *The World of the International Manager*. Allan.

International Business Week (1992) America's Hottest Exporters: Small and Mid-sized Companies are Rushing into International Markets, April 13.

Irons, K. (1991) *Managing Service Companies: Strategies for Success*. The Economist Intelligence Unit, Management Guides, September.

Kakabadse, A. (1991) *The Wealth Creators*. Kogan Page, London.

Kantor, R.M. (1983) *The Change Masters: Innovation and Entrepreneurship in the American Corporation*. New York, Simon and Schuster.

Kay, W. (1994) *The Bosses*. Piatkus, London.

Kedia, B.L. and Chokar, J. (1986) Factors Inhibiting Export Performance of Firms, *Management International Review*, **26**.

Laycock, M. (1994) Building a World-class Manufacturing Company Through Strategic Partnerships. In B. Taylor (ed.) *Successful Change Strategies: Chief Executives in Action*. Director Books.

Leadbetter, C. (1990) Europe Feeds an Appetite for Acquisitions. *Financial Times*, 20 June.

Levitt, A. and van Mesdag, M. (1987) Winging it in Foreign Markets. *Harvard Business Review*, Jan–Feb.

Levitt, Jr and Albertine, J. (1983) The Successful Entrepreneur: A Personality Profile, *Wall Street Journal*, 12 August.

Levitt, T. (1981) Marketing Intangible Products and Product Intangibles. *Harvard Business Review*, May–June.

Lloyd, B. (ed.) (1989) *Entrepreneurship: Creating and Managing New Ventures*. Pergamon Books.

Luostarinen, R. (1980) *Internationalisation of the Firm*. Helsinki School of Economics.

Mackenzie, E. A. (1992) *International Strategies for Service Businesses*. Henley Management College.

McKee, D. (1992) An Organisational Learning Approach to Product Innovation. *Journal of Product Innovation Management*, September.

Maidique, M.A. (1980) Entrepreneurs, Champions and Technological Innovation. *Sloan Management Review*, Winter.

Marsh, P. (1986) Elusive Ingredients of a High Growth Recipe. *Financial Times*, June.

van Mieghem, T. (1995) *Implementing Supplier Partnerships: How to Lower Costs and Improve Service*. Prentice Hall, Englewood Cliffs, New Jersey.

Modiano, P. and Ni-Chionna, O. (1986) Breaking into the Big Time. *Management Today*, November.

Moore, J.I. (1992) *Writers on Strategy and Strategic Management*. Penguin.

Nash, T. (1993) Britain's Unsung Heroes. *The Director*, July.

NEDC (1986) *Corporate Venturing – Strategy for Innovation and Growth*. London

Nonaka, I. and Kenney, M. (1991) Towards a New Theory of Innovation Management. *Journal of Engineering and Technology*, June.

Ohmae, K. (1987) Planting for a Global Harvest. *Harvard Business Review*, March–April.

Pearce, J.A. and Zahra, S.A. (1992) The Relative Power of CEOs and Boards of Directors: Associations with Corporate Performance. *Strategic Management Journal*, **12**, February, pp. 135–53.

Peters, T. and Waterman, R. (1982) *In Search of Excellence – Lessons from America's Best Run Corporations*. Harper & Row, New York.

Peterson, R.A. and Berger, D.G. (1971) Entrepreneurship in Organisations: Evidence from the Popular Music Industry. *Administration Science Quarterly*, March, pp. 97–106.

Porter, M. (1985) *Competitive Advantage*. New York, Free Press.

Porter, M. (1986) *Competitive Strategies*. New York, Free Press.

Robins, J.A. (1993) Organisation as Strategy: Restructuring Production in the Film Industry. *Strategic Management Journal*, **14**, 103–118.

Rock, S. (ed.) (1991) *Family Firms*. Director Books.

Rothwell, R. and Zegfeld, W. (1982) *Innovation and the Small and Medium Sized Firm*. Frances Pinter, London.

Russell, R.D. and Russell, C.J. (1992) Organisational Norms, Environmental Uncertainty and Entrepreneurial Strategy. *Journal of Management*, December.

Schein, E.H. (1985) *Organisational Culture and Leadership*. Jossey-Bass.

Schon, D.E. (1971) *Beyond the Stable State*. Temple Smith, London, p. 67.

Segal, Quince, Wicksteed and Fraunhofer Institute (1987) *New Technology Based Firms ... in West Germany and the United Kingdom*. Anglo-German Foundation, London.

Segebarth, K. (1990) Some Aspects of the International Trade in Services: An Empirical Approach. *The Services Industries Journal*, **10**, No. 2.

Siegel, R., Siegel, E. and MacMillan, I.C. (1993) Characteristics Distinguishing High Growth Ventures, *Journal of Business Venturing*, **8**, 169–180.

Simon, R. P. *et al.* (1992) *Communacopia: A Digital Communication Bounty*, Goldman Sachs & Co.

Slatter, S. (1987) *Corporate Recovery: Successful Turnaround Strategies and their Implementation.* Penguin.

Slatter, S. (1992) *Gambling on Growth*, John Wiley.

State, R. (1989) Organisational Learning: The Key to Management Innovation. *Sloan Management Review*, Spring.

Stoner, C. (1987) Distinctive Competence and Competitive Advantage. *Journal of Small Business Management*, **25** (2), 33–39.

Swords-Isherwood (1984) *The Process of Innovation – A Study of Companies in Canada, the United States and the United Kingdom.* British North American Committee, October.

Taylor, B. (ed.) (1988) *Strategic Planning, The Chief Executive and the Board.* Pergamon.

Taylor, B. (1994) *Successful Change Strategies: Chief Executives in Action.* Director Books, Hemel Hempstead.

Taylor, B., Gilinsky, A. and Hilmi, A. (1987) *Strategy and Leadership in Growth Companies.* Anglo-German Foundation, London.

Taylor, B. and Harrison, J. (1990) *The Manager's Casebook of Business Strategy.* Butterworth–Heinemann, Oxford.

Tesar, G. and Tarleton, J. (1982) *Comparison of Wisconsin and Virginia Small and Medium Sized Exporters.* In M. Czinkota and G. Tesar (eds) *Exporter Management.* Praeger.

Thorn, N. (1990) Innovation Management in Small and Medium-Sized Firms. *Management International Review*, 2nd Quarter.

Todd, A. and Taylor, B. (1993) The Baby Sharks: Strategies of Britain's Supergrowth Companies. *Long Range Planning*, **26**, April, pp. 69–77.

Vrakking, W.J. (1990) The Innovative Organisation, *Long Range Planning*, **23**, April, pp. 94–102.

Weitzen, S. (1991) *Hypergrowth: Applying the Success Formula of Today's Fastest Growing Companies.* Wiley, New York.

Wyn Griffith, M. and Taylor, B. (1994) Entrepreneurs in Entertainment: Putting on the Top Hat. *Long Range Planning*, **27** (6), December, pp. 96–107.

Young, J., Hamill, C. Wheeler, J.R. and Davies, (1989) *International Market Entry and Development: Strategies and Management.* Harvester Wheatsheaf, Herts.

Zahra, S.A. and Pearce, J.A. (1990) Determinants of Boards of Directors' Strategic Involvement, *European Management Journal*, **8**, 2.

3i/Cranfield European Enterprise Centre (1994) *European Enterprise Index.* Cranfield School of Management.

Index